LIAM BECKETT was born in Ballymoney, County Antrim. A plumber by trade, he played football for Crusaders and Coleraine in the Irish League, as well as for Drogheda in the League of Ireland, before moving into management. In 1988 he became Robert Dunlop's mechanic, manager and mentor, a partnership that ended only with Dunlop's tragic death at the North West 200 in 2008. Beckett is a sports pundit on BBC Radio Ulster and writes a weekly football column for the *Sunday Life*. He is involved with a number of local charities, and is a patron of both the Harry Gregg Foundation and the Compass Advocacy Network, and an ambassador for the Samaritans. In 2017 he was awarded an MBE for services to sport and to the voluntary sector in Northern Ireland.

FULL THROTTLE

ROBERT DUNLOP, ROAD RACING AND ME

LIAM BECKETT

·THE·
BLACK
·STAFF·
PRESS

First published in 2016 by Blackstaff Press
an imprint of Colourpoint Creative Ltd
Colourpoint House
Jubilee Business Park
21 Jubilee Road
Newtownards BT23 4YH

Reprinted with corrections, 2019

Typeset by KT Designs, Newton-le-Willows, England

Printed and bound by Martins the Printers, Berwick upon Tweed

A CIP catalogue for this book is available from the British Library

ISBN 978 0 85640 974 5

www.blackstaffpress.com

Follow Liam on Twitter: @liam_beckett

To my late mum, Maud

Contents

One
Tough start

My early life was tough. We lived in a small single-storey house with a thatched roof in Ballymoney that we rented from a local farmer. When I was just two and my brother was six my father, Jim, took ill and later passed away at the Robinson Hospital as the result of a brain haemorrhage. My mother had become a widow with two sons to look after while she was still in her early twenties.

Sadly I don't remember anything about my father so everything I do know I have learned from his family and friends. His nickname was Dusty and he was extremely skilful with his hands. Dad made all the furniture we owned and inscribed his name on each piece, which enabled him to identify his work when he was attending the joinery workshop at the technical college in Ballymoney at night. Sometimes when I felt lonely in later years I would look at his name on the back of our furniture and think about him; it filled me with pride to see his name on something that he had made himself. He was apparently handy with his mitts as well and had a reputation as someone who wouldn't back out of a confrontation. My uncle Bill used to tell me that my father had a very simple philosophy in life: 'Always show respect to those who deserve it, but never take shit from an arsehole.' I've carried that attitude throughout my life because it struck a chord with me.

My father came from a large, hard-working family from Ballywattick on the outskirts of Ballymoney. His parents were Willie and Ethel and he had three brothers, Bill, Harry and Alan, and two sisters, Ethel and Kathleen. They helped us as much as they could immediately after dad's death but I was always closer to my mother's side of the family; they seemed to be around more when I was growing up and I spent more time in their company. As time went by, I began to lose touch with my father's family and contact with them became increasingly rare as I grew older. I felt disappointed and let down by them, especially around the time of my mother's death when they were very conspicuous by their absence.

We were very much a working-class family and times were hard. Growing up without our father gave my brother Lawrence and I an insight into the reality of life and how tough it can be; we knew from an early age what it was like to have to make the best of what you had and we didn't have much in those early days. There were certainly no luxuries in the Beckett household, and my mother worked as a cleaner for a local family, the Smyths, who lived at Finvoy Road, in an effort to make ends meet. She also worked as a farm labourer for our landlord, Gerry McAfee, and I can recall many nights when my brother and I watched from the bedroom window of our little cottage as she gathered potatoes in the glow of tractor lights in the field beside our house. Given our circumstances, she had no choice but to work every available hour to provide the basics for us, particularly when extra cash was needed for our birthdays or at Christmas. Mum would never have let us go without presents and she would work even harder around these times. She was very young to be left on her own to raise two boys, but she raised us to the very best of her ability, and we had the greatest respect for her. Looking back, I am immensely proud of how she coped.

A small, thatched cottage may sound idyllic but, believe me, it was anything but. I can still hear the sound of the rats that scurried around in the thatch as we lay in bed at night. We had no electricity and at night we relied on old Tilly lamps, which ran on paraffin fuel, to provide light. Any cooking was done over an open fire and we were washed in a tin bath. My mother heated some water over the fire – just enough to take the chill out of the water – and poured it into the bath. At the back of the house we had what was known as a dry toilet, which was merely a wooden bench with a large hole on it and a tin bucket underneath. Once the bucket became full, one of us had the unenviable task of emptying the contents into a hole in the garden. I'm sure our garden must have resembled a minefield.

Although my father had made our beds and wardrobes while attending night classes at Ballymoney Technical College, he wasn't around long enough to add other bits and pieces of furniture to our home and my mother had to improvise. Our bedside cabinets, for example, were old onion boxes that she picked up from the greengrocers in town. Mum made little net curtains to cover the opening of the boxes at the front whilst a divider inside served as a makeshift shelf; they certainly did the job for us.

With no television in those early days, we were left to make our own fun. Much of our playtime was spent outside in the fields or down by the river near our house, which is known locally as the Ballymoney Burn. It's a place where I spent lots of time when I was growing up and it's where I learnt to swim. I took my own children when they were younger; I've also taken my grandchildren to the same spot, and fondly recounted my memories of summer days spent fishing and swimming. We had friends who lived nearby, most of whom were little better off than we were ourselves, and we used to have a great time stealing apples from the orchard in a neighbouring large country estate or playing football together. Without question, football was the one activity that kept us all amused for hours on end. It was affordable because all you needed was a ball and somewhere to kick it. We used our coats for goalposts and, once we had decided on the teams, we'd play all day long, without a single care in the world. It wouldn't be until Mum shouted, 'Supper's ready' that we'd pause for a break. Once we'd been fed and watered we'd be straight back outside and the game would continue with just as much enthusiasm until darkness crept in.

I adored football from an early age and I soon realised that I was pretty good at it. Much to the annoyance of the older lads I was able to dribble the ball around them and find the back of the net with a fair degree of regularity, though in the early days my preferred role was keeping nets as we called it. I imagined that I was Harry Gregg, the great Manchester United goalkeeper, who only lived down the road in Coleraine. He was my idol – when I was young, I never could have imagined that one day I would be able to count him as a close friend.

Each day I'd walk the two miles to the Model Primary School in Ballymoney and repeat the journey in the afternoon. Football, of course, was a big attraction at school and it gave me the opportunity to test my skills against other boys around the same age as myself as well as with the older lads. Generally speaking, I was able to take on and beat most of my opponents when I had the ball at my feet. There were some decent players at school, including the late Coleraine, Arsenal and Linfield winger, Shaun Dunlop. There was one lad, though, who was a cut above the rest: Chris Moore. He is now a leading investigative journalist and television documentary producer. I see him quite often and always remind him of the qualities he showed as a very young footballer at primary school in Ballymoney. I have no doubt that Chris could have at least played at senior level in the Irish

4

League – but his family moved away to Scotland while he was still at primary school and that was that. A couple of the teachers noticed my early promise, and took me to one side during a kick-about at lunchtime to tell me to make sure I didn't waste the talent I had been born with. For the first time in my life I felt equal to the other lads at school.

Being honest, I was never a boy who enjoyed school and I was always much happier when I was playing in the fields at home or kicking a football with my friends. Secondary school soon loomed large on the horizon and at the age of eleven I became enrolled at Ballymoney High School or the intermediate, as we called it. I was a country boy, and I didn't thrive in large crowds, but I had to bite the bullet like everyone else. Thankfully many of my friends from primary school were also heading to the intermediate, so I wasn't going alone. We didn't have the money, and anyway I didn't have any desire, to try to get a place at the town's leading grammar school, Dalriada.

I was never really happy at school and secondary school was no different. There are times now when I wish that I had listened more intently in class but I always preferred the joinery or metalwork classes to the academic teaching – perhaps working with my hands was something I inherited from my father. I think I suffered from a bit of an inferiority complex because the majority of children at school had two parents. Those feelings weren't helped by the fact that I received free meal vouchers at school and I always felt embarrassed handing that red ticket over to the dinner lady in the canteen. Sometimes I was aware of the other children sniggering in the background and, as the days and months wore on, I began to dread lunchtime.

I began to realise that I had a bit of a short temper and if anyone dangled the bait in front of me, the chances were that I'd snap. I'd have been eleven or twelve when I started getting into fights at school and there were plenty of them. Gone were the days when I'd accept the other lads poking fun at me and

5

we generally sorted out any differences with our fists. Back then if you had a disagreement with someone it was sorted out in a one-on-one bare knuckle scrap: it was always man to man and you wouldn't have had large groups of boys ganging up to give one person a beating, which seems to happen a lot these days. We would fight in the cloakrooms or in the playground and often organised fights after school hours. The so-called hard men would head to a pre-arranged location followed by large groups of their friends and a bunch of hangers-on, who formed a 'ring' for the fighters. It was always a fair fight, and only ended when someone admitted they'd had enough. I was involved in my fair share of these fights and I realised that I was that bit better with my fists than most of the others. Some fights lasted a few seconds, others went on for much longer and I recall one really tough guy in particular that I fought for over an hour. On that occasion, I think we accepted that the fight had been a draw. My late father had also been handy with his hands apparently and perhaps that, coupled with a relatively tough upbringing, stood me in good stead in later life in terms of being able to look after myself.

As the years passed, I remained resolute in my dislike of school. In one term alone I skipped about forty days. I used to take a detour in the morning to a big tree, which I climbed up, and where I stayed until three o'clock when it was home time. I'd survive on these big toffee penny chews, which were wrapped in green paper and kept me chewing away contentedly; they were about the size of a Milky Way and my jaws would be aching when I eventually got home in the evening. The school's truant officer, Harry Scott, was regularly out and about looking for pupils absent from school and, although I had a few close shaves, he didn't catch me once.

In 1965, around the time that I started secondary school, my mum managed to get a full-time job in the canteen at Corfield's camera factory in Ballymoney. We also received the offer of an end terrace house at Gate End on the edge of Ballymoney; a normal two-up, two-down dwelling but it felt like the lap of luxury to us. We had electricity, and a modern flush toilet in the back yard, situated around twenty-five yards from the back door; we even had a doorbell. When it was dark I would leave the light on in the scullery and the back door open as I made my way through the yard to the toilet, then I'd sit 'clocking' on the loo with the door ajar.

I spent many hours in the yard kicking a ball against the wall and it helped my technique tremendously; rarely does a ball return to your feet the same way twice when you hit it against a wall. Money was still scarce, but we were going up in the world, and I was so proud of my mum. We bought furniture and lino floor covering on tick from a gentleman who owned a furniture business in the town, Albert Shirlow, who was kind to us. It was nice being able to add bits and pieces to the house, but when we splashed out on an old second-hand black and white television set, I thought we'd won the pools. It was a slot television, the type that was coin-operated. The picture was never stable: one moment you'd be watching cowboys and Indians engaged in battle in the middle of the screen and the next thing they'd disappear through the top of the television, only to reappear at the bottom of the screen, still fighting away. I was as proud as punch though, and I never made my friends any the wiser that the picture quality was terrible.

One perk of mum's new job at the factory canteen was that she was permitted to bring home any leftovers and basically that's what we lived on; the only time we saw real meat it was running through a field. Quite often she'd bring home a saucepan half full of uneaten rice and that would be our supper. We never went hungry, though – Mum always saw to it that Lawrence and I had enough to eat. We really looked forward to Saturday mornings when the bread man called at our house. Mum allowed us to have one bun each and we always plumped for the same choice, Paris buns, which had big lumps of sugar on top. It was probably the highlight of our week. Although we were short on many things, love from our mum wasn't one of them: she sacrificed everything for us.

In July 1964, my mum remarried. Her husband was a man called James O'Brien, who lived just outside the town. He was a quiet man, a motor mechanic by trade, and Lawrence and I were very happy for them both. But money, or the lack of it, was always a problem and when I left school I took on a job as a message boy, delivering fruit and vegetables for a shop called Moores, which was owned by decent people with very strong Christian beliefs. I think I earned something like ten bob a week for six days' work, which included working all day on a Saturday: probably about fifty pence in today's money. It wasn't much, but when you consider that a bag of chips would have been a shilling back then (ten pence today), it was welcome pocket money for a young boy. If mum needed any of the money, then I handed it over without question and I kept what was left, but usually I was able to keep the lot.

I met my first proper girlfriend, Elizabeth Kennedy, around this time, when I was about fourteen. She came from the village of Dunaghy, not far from Ballymoney. She tragically lost her life in a car accident one evening when she was returning from a dance in Ballycastle. Elizabeth, who was only a teenager, was a passenger in a car that was involved in a head-on collision. It was an awful shock and – because I was too young to remember my father's death – it was the first big setback of my life, but it wasn't to be the last.

Two
When football became serious

Sport, thankfully, always offered me some respite from the daily grind. I never mooched off school when sport was on the timetable. I was achieving success in football, and it offered me a chance to perform on the field, to feel equal to the other lads. In 1965, when I was fourteen, I was selected for the Northern Ireland Schoolboy team. I was overjoyed and immensely proud, although I still didn't own a pair of football boots, which was causing me some concern. I needn't have worried as my family all clubbed together to buy me a gleaming set of boots for £3 from Bishops shoe shop in Coleraine.

When I was the legal leaving age, the committee of the schoolboy team tried to convince my mother that I should attend school at least one day a week once I'd left to remain eligible for selection for the schoolboys team; but as soon as I received an offer of a plumbing apprenticeship, my mind was made up, and I left school. I wish now that I had taken advantage of the further schoolboy international opportunities that were available to me then – but, of course, it wasn't the footballing side of the bargain that turned me, it was the prospect of more school. Once my apprenticeship began, football went on to the backburner, although I sometimes managed to squeeze in the odd Saturday morning game for our local YMCA team.

Around this time, my home life changed too. My girlfriend June and I had been going out together since I was about fifteen, and two years later, she fell pregnant. June lived just around the corner in a housing estate called Westgate. Her family and my mum were in agreement that we should get married, so we duly tied the knot in what was known in those days as a shotgun wedding. Soon after we rented a little house at Milltown, at the bottom end of the town in Ballymoney. Our respective families helped us to kit out our new home in time for the birth of our first child, Louise. Our second baby, whom we named Lawrence after my brother, was born not long after. I doted on Louise and Lawrence, and still do, and June was a fine woman, a good and hard-working wife, but for whatever reason I soon became discontent. I started to venture out more on my own with my mates and I was quickly growing restless with married life. I can see now I was too young and immature for marriage at that point in my life.

One night, in 1971, I was playing in a summer league match for a Coleraine side in Garvagh in County Londonderry, not too far from my hometown of Ballymoney. They were a handy team that included a lad called Colm McFeeley from Coleraine, who lived in Belfast at the time. Colm also played Irish League football at the time for Crusaders FC and, after the game, he came over and asked me if I'd be interested in playing for Crusaders. The following Saturday I played a game for the reserves team, which also included the one and only Norman Pavis. I played quite well and the next Tuesday night I was asked to sign for the Crues as soon as I reported for training.

Suddenly, I rediscovered my hunger for football and although I was a dyed-in-the-wool country boy joining a team in Belfast city, I was made to feel right at home by everyone at the Shore

Road club. Within seven days of signing, I was given a chance to play in the first team alongside Irish League legends like John McPolin and Walter McFarland. I was a part-time professional, still working away in my plumbing job, but I felt an immense feeling of pride and I couldn't wait to get home to tell my family the news. I was handed my first team kit and told to report to Seaview on Saturday with the rest of the squad. I was so thrilled I could have walked the whole way to Belfast that day. I fully expected to be sitting in the grandstand or at best on the bench, because in that era of football, there was only one substitute player per team. As we arrived at the ground, I did the same as the other players and took a walk up the pitch, where I was joined by the manager, Billy Johnston. He pulled me to one side and said, 'You're starting, Liam. You'll play inside forward to Sammy Pavis.' I nearly dropped on the spot on hearing the news: my uncle Jock had taken me to Windsor Park when I was a kid to watch his beloved Linfield and I'd watched many times as Pavis – an absolute legend in Irish football – scored goals for fun for the Blues. Now here I was, preparing to play alongside Sammy, and I was absolutely starstruck. I performed fairly well in that first game, and I held my place on the first team throughout that season. Billy Johnston signed Jackie Fullerton not long after me, and he became my best friend from that day forward.

We were primed for a big year in 1973, and the whole squad worked tirelessly during pre-season that year. The season that unfolded went down in history as one of the greatest years ever for Crusaders FC as we clinched the biggest prize in Irish League Football for the very first time, plus the Carlsberg Cup, and had a glorious march to the league title. The celebrations went on for days. Of all the medals I have picked up during my career, the Irish League title takes pride of place. We made history that day.

I couldn't have been happier at Crusaders but my home life was a different story altogether. My marriage was becoming more strained by the day. It was all my own fault – I wasn't there for my wife and family. As soon as I came home from work, I was off to Belfast for training, rarely returning home before 11 p.m., even later on match nights when we went out for a few beers after the game. So when Billy Johnston told me that the club had received an offer for me from Drogheda United, and I told June about it, she just shrugged her shoulders. However, my mum was worried about me travelling back and forth across the border because the Troubles were at their height, and the border areas were always especially dangerous, but she thought that I should at least go and meet them.

When I met the Drogheda manager, John Cowan, and their scout, Arthur 'Mousey' Brady, I was impressed by their vision for the club, and I was blown away by the quality of players they had already signed. I put pen to paper on a three-year deal. This new chapter in my career also marked the end of my marriage. It was a sad time: June had been my childhood sweetheart and we had two beautiful children. I still saw as much of the kids as I could until they moved away to England a few years later.

Playing for Drogheda brought many new experiences, especially for a Protestant – a tour of the local chapel to see Saint Oliver Plunkett's head; some small-scale smuggling of butter from north to south by a team-mate as an earner on the side; sitting among my team-mates – the only Prod on the bus – as they sang rebel songs; and countless trips in the minibus from Belfast to Drogheda for matches and training. I thrived during my time there and the experience was invaluable to me – I even managed to score a couple of memorable goals, despite my position as a defender. Sadly my stint in the League of Ireland was to end in heartbreak.

Back in the seventies, summer league football was extremely popular. As paid professionals, we weren't permitted to participate in any of these games outside the regular season under the terms of our contracts. That summer, in 1974, I played with my dear friend Danny Trainor for Ardoyne Celtic in the Buncrana Cup. A few weeks later I was also invited to play for a local Ballymoney side in another big summer cup competition called the Hughes Cup, which was held in my hometown. The organisers had asked me if I'd be able to bring any of my senior team-mates to take part and, as soon as I mentioned it to the Belfast contingent of Drogheda players – Danny Trainor, Geordie O'Halloran and Gerry Brammeld – they had no hesitation in pledging their commitment. We lost our game, and afterwards we decided to go for a couple of beers before the Belfast lads headed home. There were two carloads of us and we went to the Bridge Bar in Dunloy, a few miles outside Ballymoney.

Everyone was relaxed and in good form and we had good craic as usual, although I didn't have any beer as I was on driving duty that evening. A friend of mine, Jimmy Wilson, had agreed to drive some of the players to the bar in his car so he too stuck to soft drinks. When we left the bar, Jimmy Wilson was driving the car in front of me with Danny Trainor in the front passenger seat and Gerry Brammeld in the rear. I was driving my car with Geordie O'Halloran, Paddy Dunlop and Joe McVicker as passengers. As both our cars approached a built-up area on the outskirts of Ballymoney, I became aware of a car with its lights on heading out of town and travelling in the opposite direction. It appeared to stop in the crown of the road and wait there and I assumed that the driver was going to turn right after we had passed by. To my horror, just as we approached the car, it turned right, into the path of Jimmy Wilson, who ploughed straight into it in what was virtually a head-on collision. There was a massive shower of sparks and smoke as the two vehicles smashed together. I somehow managed to steer my way around the mangled wreckage in the middle of the road before slamming on the brakes. We all jumped out and ran back towards the scene, which was a vision of utter carnage. What I saw that day will remain with me for the rest of my life and I was in a state of complete shock and panic. By this time, a few other cars had stopped and people were screaming at the horror before them. In what seemed like no time at all, the emergency services arrived at the scene. From what I could see, it appeared as though only one person out of the five who were travelling in both cars were showing any signs of life and that was Gerry Brammeld, who was riding in the back seat of Jimmy Wilson's car. There were no seatbelts in those days and that only served to diminish the chances of survival. I could see Jimmy and big Danny Trainor slumped in the front seats, while I was pretty sure the two people in the other car were dead.

We had been told to stay well back from the scene by the police but I could hear the medical personnel say that they had found a pulse on Jimmy Wilson. Members of the Fire Brigade were working tirelessly with cutting equipment to free everyone from the mangled wreckage but one of the police officers informed me that both of the persons in the other car had indeed been killed instantly. I was sat on the footpath in utter shock, trying to comprehend what had happened. Finally I saw that Jimmy Wilson and Gerry Brammeld had been freed and they were put in the back of an ambulance, which sped away from the scene with sirens blaring and lights blazing. I was unable to see Danny Trainor, though, and my worst fears were confirmed when someone put their hand on my shoulder and said, 'Liam, the other big lad didn't make it.' I remember thinking it couldn't be true and that they must have made a mistake because Danny was built like a brick wall, but the reality of the situation hit home when they led me down the footpath to where a body was lying on the ground covered with a blanket. It was Danny, of course, and I broke down. How could this giant of a man, an absolutely superb footballer, be dead? It felt like a bad dream but sadly it was all too real.

I learned that the victims travelling in the other car were an elderly local couple who lived across the road not far from the scene of the accident. They were returning home from a trip into the town and had unfortunately seemed to misjudge the speed and distance of Jimmy Wilson's car as it approached them. They were a lovely couple who came from a highly respected family and the whole incident was just such an unbearable tragedy. I was taken to hospital myself and treated for shock along with the others who were travelling in my car. At the Route Hospital in Ballymoney, we became aware that the doctors were fighting to save the lives of Gerry Brammeld and Jimmy Wilson. My mind was in overdrive and all I could think about was Danny's family because I'd been at his house earlier that day and as we left he had rubbed the heads of his young sons and said, 'See you later, kids.' I couldn't process how a simple night out playing football and having a couple of beers afterwards had ended so cruelly, with three people confirmed dead and another two critically injured.

The following few days were totally heartbreaking with the funerals of the local elderly couple and Danny Trainor bringing into focus the overwhelming sense of loss experienced by the friends and family of all three. I was a complete emotional wreck and found it all very hard to deal with because I was still only in my twenties. It was a dark time in my life but one beacon of light was the recoveries of Jimmy Wilson and Gerry Brammeld, who thankfully both managed to pull through. Gerry made a miraculous recovery to the point where he was able to play Irish League football at Senior level once more, although Jimmy was left with a limp as a result of the horrendous leg injuries he suffered in the crash. I must pay tribute to the medical team at the former Route Hospital and the emergency personnel who did such a wonderful job at the crash scene: I'll be forever indebted to them.

The mental scars of that terrible day have remained with me ever since and my heart was shattered as I sat in Danny Trainor's living room in Ardoyne in Belfast after his funeral, not far from the Shamrock Club where he used to take me for a few beers after we'd played a home game for Drogheda United. His two sons and young wife were inconsolable and the burden of his untimely death seemed too much to bear.

Eventually, I was able to move on with my life and return to playing football again. I had met a girl who was to become my wife. Both being from the small town of Ballymoney, I'd known Gillian Tweed's family for a long time, but I met Gillian properly in 1974, when she had only just turned sixteen. I was twenty-three and her family were concerned about her relationship with me because I'd already been married. So things were obviously tough enough for us at the start.

As it turned out, the concerns of Gillian's family over our relationship were the least of my worries at the time because disaster loomed around the corner once more. In October 1974, I had accepted an offer to play for a team called Belfast Dockers in a challenge game in the Republic of Ireland against Dublin Dockers. Effectively, it was illegal for me to compete in this match under the terms of my contract with Drogheda, but my team-mate Geordie O'Halloran and former Crusaders player Joe Patterson were also playing, so I agreed to take part. Our team also included a top quality footballer who only had one arm, Belfast man Jimmy Hasty, who was a tall, elegant player and a superb talent despite his disability. We made the trip south to take on Dublin Dockers and won the game before embarking on a drinking binge all the way home. Big Jimmy was wearing a suede cowboy hat on the trip back and we had some laugh, with all the lads in great form. A few days later I received a phone call that shook me to the core with the news that Jimmy Hasty had been shot dead on his way to work at the docks in Belfast. I was numb and in a state of shock, especially since this tragedy had happened so soon after the fatal car accident that had claimed the life of my team-mate Danny Trainor. The big lad that I had shared a dressing room with many times had been cut down in a hail of gunfire early one morning as our country continued to be ripped apart by sectarianism and terrorism. It was a needless waste of life but sadly Jimmy's death at the hands of masked gunmen was an all too regular occurrence during the Troubles in Northern Ireland. But thankfully football served as a common denominator amongst the bullets, bombs and bloodshed and helped unite both sides of the community during the times when it felt as though all was lost.

Understandably, my mother and many within my family were concerned for my safety as I continued to play football across the border. Often, I made the return trip from Belfast to Drogheda four times a week, and they felt that I was asking for trouble. I didn't give too much thought to it at the time, but now I can see they had a valid point. I began to wonder if perhaps it was again time for a change in my career and my relationship with Gillian was a big factor in this. I was all too aware that her family had major doubts over whether she would have much of a future with me – a situation that wasn't helped by the fact that I was playing for a team miles away and was more often absent than at home.

As I began to deliberate over my future, the decision was effectively taken out of my hands when I received a phone call from two friends of mine from Ballymoney, former Coleraine FC legends Ivan Murray and Johnny McCurdy. They informed me of some exciting news: they were set to take over as joint managers of the Bannsiders in place of footballing great Bertie Peacock, who was going to announce his retirement. I agreed to meet them both the following night and I was sold on their plans for the club immediately. Bertie had assembled a magnificent team at the Coleraine Showgrounds, which was more than capable of challenging for Irish League honours. I remained as hungry as ever for more medals and the offer seemed to tick a lot of boxes, not least because I lived ten minutes down the road from the club. I had fallen madly in love with Gillian and really wanted to make the relationship work, so bringing an end to the frequent trips to Drogheda and the many weekends away from her made perfect sense.

My mind was made up and I contacted my manager at Drogheda United, John Cowan, who was very understanding over my situation, but warned me that the board of directors might not be so receptive to my request for a transfer. John recommended that I ask my mum to write a letter to them outlining her fears in relation to my safety in light of the spiral of sectarian violence. Mum had no hesitation in doing just that and not long after we posted the letter, I received a phone call to say that the club had agreed to place me on the transfer list, but there would be a fee to secure my services. I feared that this would prove a significant stumbling block in the way of me joining Coleraine, but they had a terrific supporters club based in Ballymoney, headed by a local shop owner called Robert Anderson. Coleraine had asked the club for financial assistance to secure my transfer and Robert visited me at home to confirm that I was serious over completing the move. 'If you're sure you want to come, then we'll find the money to pay the transfer fee,' he told me. I was absolutely delighted and indebted to Robert and Ballymoney C.F.C Supporters Club for their faith in me. Within a relatively short space of time, Drogheda and Coleraine agreed the terms of my transfer and I was clear to join the most successful team I would ever play for. Although I was relieved to be resuming my football career at home, I was sad at the same time to be leaving Drogheda after two years. I had made so many good friends and I missed them all greatly, especially the Belfast lads. I was treated so well by everyone at Drogheda United and have many precious memories of my time there.

A new era dawned for me at Coleraine, where there was an excellent side packed with accomplished players, many of whom hailed from the surrounding area. To cap it all, the club had a wonderful chairman in the late, great Jack Doherty. He always did the best he could for all the players at Coleraine and he was held in the utmost regard. When you joined the team back then, you were joining a family, and Jack was like a father to us all. We would have walked over hot coals for him.

My career at Coleraine was one big success story. In 1975, the prospect of adding the prestigious Irish Cup to my other medals was driving me on. Put simply, we had the best team in the country that year and we cruised to the final of the Irish Cup with very little fuss. Only the mighty Linfield stood in our way. The playing surface at Ballymena was like a snooker table that day, but there was a gale-force wind blowing down the centre of the pitch. In the end, we ground out a draw, and had forced a replay, which took place four days later on 23 April. Although we were able to field a stronger side, thanks to key players who were available again after suspension, the match ended in another stalemate, this time a scoreless draw.

So the destination of the 1975 Irish Cup remained undecided and both teams gathered themselves once again for a second replay. With both sides so obviously evenly matched, it was going to take something special to break the deadlock. Another punishing match unfolded in front of the expectant crowd at the Ballymena Showgrounds and, as fate would have it, we scored the only goal to finally settle the matter and secure the coveted Irish Cup. Jim 'Chang' Smith was the hero of the hour as he struck to break Linfield's hearts and send the Coleraine fans delirious. I'd only been at my new club for a short time, but already I'd won the only other senior medal within Irish League football that I really desired. My late father would have been so proud and I wished he had been there with me, but I was thankful my mother and Gillian were there to see it and they were just ecstatic. My uncle Jock was also there, but as a diehard Blues fan he detested Coleraine and he didn't speak to me for quite a few weeks afterwards: if I was wearing a Coleraine shirt, I was as bad as the rest of them in his eyes. As for the post-match celebration following our magnficient Irish Cup triumph, I remember very little about the weekend. I was never a big drinker, but I must have consumed a full year's quota of alcohol after the match and probably lay in bed suffering the effects for about three days afterwards.

We had qualified for the European Cup Winners' Cup competition as a result of our success and landed a plum draw against the crack West German side Eintracht Frankfurt. We slumped to a 4–1 defeat at the Coleraine Showgrounds, which left us wondering what lay in store in the return leg of the first-round tie in Frankfurt two weeks later. These European away games were in effect little more than a bonus for our success at local level back home because very rarely did an Irish League team have any real hopes of causing an upset against one of the big teams. The biggest majority of European sides were full-time professionals with some of the world's greatest names on their books, so the gulf in class was obviously massive. In saying that, no matter how high the odds against us, we always strove to give a good account of ourselves. The game itself was little more than a damage limitation exercise and although we played quite well, we again lost 4-1. The pace with which they moved the ball was electrifying and it was a high tempo pass-and-move style of football, which we were simply unable to contend with.

That 1975 season also proved to be a good one for us in other competitions as we finished runners-up in the league, although I always felt that finishing second meant we were merely the first losers. I rarely look at that league medal and even though I know where I keep it, never would it enter my mind to seek it out. We won the Hennessey Gold Cup and the Ulster Cup competitions but missed out on a treble after slipping to defeat in the City Cup to Bangor, who defeated us on penalties. Bangor were a decent team but with all due respect to them, we really should have seen them off and won another final. It was a hugely disappointing loss that brought to an end our incredible unbeaten run of thirty-six games, which is a record that still stands. Coupled with a squandered opportunity to claim another medal, 10 December 1975 is a date that will rankle for the rest of my days. Perhaps that wonderful sequence of victories will never be beaten, although my gut feeling is that someday it will. One thing is certain though, it will take a very good side to accomplish such a feat because we were a crack side in '75, despite some major setbacks along the way.

During the latter stages of my career, I was persistently troubled by a left groin injury. I required injections before every game during the final season to numb the pain and perhaps it was naive of me not to quit sooner, but such was my love for the game and for Coleraine that I always felt it was my duty to play through the pain barrier. I very briefly returned to Crusaders, but was persuaded by Jack Doherty, who had been so good to me, to come back to Coleraine. It was to be a short reunion, though.

Victor Hunter had taken over from Ivan and Johnny, and towards the end of his tenure the club signed a lad called Gerry Magowan, who hailed from Londonderry. It soon emerged that Magowan was out on bail at the time on a charge of being an accessory in the murder of a soldier shot dead in Londonderry. I was absolutely stunned, particularly because many of my family were or had been members of the security forces and I was lost for words that the club would sign someone who had been charged with this type of crime. I wanted answers and I confronted the chairman, Jack Doherty, and demanded to know what the hell they were playing at. In fairness, Jack was straight up with me as always and his reply to me was, 'Look, I've only just heard this myself and apparently he's not being charged with the actual shooting, but he's been accused of being a lookout.' I was unmoved and retorted, 'Same bloody thing' because to me, at that time, there was no difference in my eyes and he may as well have pulled the trigger, even though he'd only been charged and not convicted. I told Jack there was no way I'd ever share the dressing room with Magowan, never mind play alongside him because my principles simply wouldn't allow it. Jack looked at me for a moment and then told me that I'd have to submit a transfer request in writing if I wanted to leave, so I did exactly that the very next day.

The news spread like wildfire and feelings were running high within the club. At this time, the Troubles in Northern Ireland weren't quite as bad as they had been during the early seventies for example, but tension was always lurking beneath a fragile veneer. Let me make it abundantly clear that although I am a Protestant, I never had any problem whatsoever playing football with my Catholic team-mates and some of my closest friends are on the other side of the religious divide. My late mother brought me up to respect my Catholic friends and I have followed her example steadfastly throughout my life, but there was no chance that I could morally accept a suspected republican terrorist as a team-mate and my attitude would have been the same had the club signed a suspected loyalist terrorist. I put in writing my revulsion at the club's decision to sign Gerry Magowan and reiterated that I no longer wished to be involved with Coleraine FC.

Things were changing fast behind the scenes at the club following my decision to request a transfer and as the furore continued to grow around the signing, the powers that be decided to cut their losses and offload him. Although I agreed to withdraw my transfer request as a result, things didn't feel right at the showgrounds after the saga, which had left a bad taste in the mouth. It has since come to light that Gerry McGowan and the other three men arrested at the same time as him were innocent of all charges against them.

The team by that time was only a shadow of the great side we had in the early to mid-seventies and the manager, Victor Hunter, was struggling to replicate the success of previous seasons, so a lot of the hunger and desire I had was beginning to wilt. The whole situation felt like a slog and with my groin requiring injections before every game, I was really finding it difficult to commit properly. My lack of drive was completely foreign to me.

I was also kept busy by my plumbing business and by our young family. When Gillian and I first set up home together, we lived in a small, first-floor flat, which was located halfway along Main Street in Ballymoney. It was a very modest home, but we made do as best we could. I was still a young plumber and my mediocre wages back then were quickly swallowed up by my maintenance commitments to my two children from my first marriage, plus my utility bills and of course the expense involved in running a car, which wasn't a particularly good one at that. I had no idea of the real value of money at that time in my life and my earnings from plumbing and football never seemed to be enough to cover all my outgoings. I suppose it would be fair to say I was flat broke most of the time. In fact, when Gillian and I pooled our combined resources, I actually found myself £14 in the red. But again I was very lucky – Gillian was very hardworking and really put in the hours as a machinist at a local factory to make ends meet. She also very often went without to make sure the family came first.

There is one memory that really stands out from this time; a day when I was absolutely famished. I went to the larder and, to my dismay, all that was on offer was a solitary tin of spaghetti. I detest spaghetti – it reminds me of nothing more than worms dipped in tomato sauce. However, on this occasion, I had no other option. As I chewed and swallowed it down, my stomach was heaving. Although, thanks be to God, our financial situation has improved since those days, I have never forgotten what it was like to have nothing and it is these kinds of memories that ensure my feet remain firmly on the ground. And needless to say, never again has a strand of spaghetti entered my mouth.

We moved on from the flat in Main Street before too long – we built our own house in 1977, and then our daughter Janice was born in 1978, followed by Lynsey in '83, William in '86 and Robert in 1990.

Football was beginning to drop further down my list of priorities but then Victor Hunter was replaced as manager by my old friend and team-mate Dessie Dickson, which had the effect of extending my involvement with Coleraine. Dickie was a legend as a player at the club and I opted to stay put and give him all the support I could as he was a rookie in the role. He started his tenure strongly and didn't take any nonsense from anyone, but he had inherited what I still consider to be a poor side. In truth, though, my love affair with football was over and at the early age of thirty the curtain came down on my playing days for good.

Three
Full throttle

I'd always loved football and I'd always loved road racing. My first trip to the North West 200 wasn't the best introduction, though. When I was about eight, my brother Lawrence and I and a few of his mates were hanging around at my grandmother's house in Balnamore, on the outskirts of Ballymoney. One of the older lads came up with the bright idea that we should all go to the North West 200 on the Saturday of that week. With a quick show of hands it was decided that we would make up packed lunches and take a couple of big bottles of lemonade with us and leave early on the Saturday morning, walking the whole way to Portstewart, a distance of about twelve miles. No other mode of transport was available to us in those days.

I stayed overnight on the Friday at my grandmother's so we could make an early start and I woke up the next morning bubbling with excitement. I always loved it when I could tag along with my big brother Lawrence and the older lads, even though they were only about twelve. I vividly remember going into my granny's wee scullery in her end terrace house on the Grey Row in Balnamore to make my lunch. I cut myself a few big, thick slices of bread from one of those unsliced plain loaves that you saw a lot in those days. I slapped on the butter and planted a sliced home-grown tomato inside each and every sandwich and sprinkled on some salt and pepper to make the thickest sandwiches I had ever seen. I packed them into a brown paper bag and rolled the neck of it up to form a makeshift handle so I could carry it with me. I pulled on my jeans and a jumper, a light jacket and a pair of well worn gutties and was all set for the adventure ahead. We set off and in no time at all I was complaining that my legs and feet were hurting and the expressions on the other lads' faces told me they were wondering why the hell they had agreed to allow me to go with them. My threadbare gutties were overheating big time and my feet felt like they were on fire. The older boys kept encouraging me to keep going, assuring me, 'It's not much further, just over the next hill.' I swear, I thought we were walking to the Isle of Man, it was taking so long, but several hours and a few pit-stops later, I finally saw the sea in Portstewart. The racing had already started but all I wanted to do was lie down behind a wall and eat my tomato sandwiches because by this stage in the proceedings, I was absolutely famished and exhausted. Sadly, this was when my whole world fell apart. Somewhere along the way, the arse had fallen out of my brown paper bag. The soggy tomatoes combined with the weight of those big thick slices of bread had created a hole that had allowed my lunch to escape somewhere between Balnamore and Portstewart. It dawned on me that for some miles now, I had merely been holding on to the neck of an empty paper bag. I could have cried, and in fact I may have done just that. At least the birds would have enjoyed a feast somewhere along those country roads. I didn't starve completely, though, as my brother and the other lads shared some of their lunch with me. All I really wanted to do was go home and I remember thinking, 'I'll never be back here again.' Little did I know.

Thankfully, I had some better experiences of going to races

with my uncle, Jackie Graham, who was married to my mum's sister, Sally. Jackie was Joey Dunlop's chief mechanic and is, without doubt, the most knowledgeable man I have ever met. He was an absolute mechanical engineering genius. Many of the leading race teams back in the day came to Jackie for advice. Any time he took delivery of a new machine, he'd check it over with a fine toothcomb before setting off to his workshop where he'd use his lathe and milling machines, and even modify some of the factory parts he felt could be improved. The carburettors were usually the first components to be dissected and altered as Jackie worked his magic. Both Joey and Robert trusted him implicitly and he was a massive help to both boys.

Jackie started taking me to races when I was a teenager and, in spite of my earlier tomato sandwich disaster, I was instantly smitten. When I wasn't playing football on a Saturday, I was invariably attending a road race. I admired every one of those lads out there, risking life and limb, but the Dunlops were easily my favourite racers. It was impossible to grow up in a small town like Ballymoney and not be a supporter. Those were great times in road racing, with the Armoy Armada of Joey, Joey's brother Jim Dunlop, Mervyn Robinson and big Frank Kennedy competing in fierce rivalry with the Dromara Destroyers – Ray McCullough, Brian Reid, Trevor Steele and Ian McGregor – all incredible pilots. Ireland was full of talented riders, like Sam McClements, Eddie Laycock, Phillip McCallen and Woolsey Coulter, but although I had the utmost respect for them all, I was unashamedly a Dunlop man, and I remain so to this day.

In 1988, on one of his regular visits to our house – which was in Derrykeighan, about six miles from Ballymoney – my uncle Jackie told me that Robert Dunlop was struggling to get a foothold in racing. He was living with his young wife Louise in a rented cottage on the same Enagh Road where I was born, on the outskirts of Ballymoney. Rob didn't have much room to work on his bikes but I had a large purpose-built workshop at my house for my plumbing business and I told Jackie that Robert was more than welcome to come and work on his machines at my place.

It was an offer that would change my life. In next to no time Robert had arrived with a 125cc Honda as well as an old 250cc Yamaha – which incidentally was a heap of manure – together with a few spanners lying in the arse of an old rusted toolbox. Road racing was one of my favourite sports, right up there with football. So every spare moment I got at home, between plumbing jobs, I was out in the workshop to see what Rob was at. And he wasn't backward in asking me to lend a hand. Literally, within hours of him arriving for the first time, he had assigned me a task. I had to wash down the frame of one of the bikes with a dish of petrol and a paintbrush, with Rob keeping a watchful eye and reminding me to watch the tyres. A splash of petrol with oil residue mixed through could have proved disastrous if it had managed to find its way on to the edge of one of the tyres, destroying the adhesion, so it was important to be extra careful. Washing the frame may sound a simple task, but it did have a fair degree of responsibility attached – back then, frames were prone to cracking through either metal fatigue or at the points where the frame was welded, so inspecting for hairline fractures was part of the job. Failure to spot one could be catastrophic at high speed. Rob was meticulous in the preparation of his bikes, and this was the first of many jobs – we became a great team and spent hours in my workshop, preparing the bikes for race meetings all over Ireland, with Rob's trusty old radio providing the soundtrack to our labour. It had a coat hanger wedged in to replace its broken aerial and that wee radio never cooled; it was on constantly as we fettled the bikes.

Previously, Robert had had a couple of good lads, Trevor Murphy and Kevin Trainor, giving him a hand but they both had full-time jobs, and therefore found it difficult to devote the time necessary to take Robert to the next level. I was lucky enough to be self-employed, and Robert and I gelled right from the start – from the very first day I knew our relationship was going to be special. I took to him straight away because he was a jovial character with a great sense of humour, plus he was a Jack-the-lad and was always up to all the pranks of the day. At first, I spent my spare time helping Robert; before long, I found myself making the time to help him, and my days and nights revolved around the work on the bikes. And after just a few weeks, I found myself all kitted out in a Shell Oils boiler suit as I set off for that year's North West 200 with Robert.

Because we were from the same town, and just nine years apart in age, I knew Robert a bit before I began working with him, and I had watched and admired him racing many times. But it was only once I'd started to spend more time with him that I realised that he lacked real self-belief and focus. I knew that Rob had tremendous natural talent – that comes pretty much engrained in the DNA of the Dunlops – but he had very little confidence. His elder brother Joey was very well established in the sport by this time, and had an army of followers, not to mention countless helpers and assistants who worshipped his every move. He was also winning major races, while Robert was only having the odd success at the smaller national road races, and occasionally venturing over to England to compete on the short circuits when he'd gathered up enough money to fill his old van with red diesel. A lot of the young Irish riders who crossed the Irish Sea to race were mainly looking for a good drinking session and a bit of craic: their priorities were all wrong with the racing coming second on their agenda.

Robert fitted into that category and when I challenged him on why he seemed happy enough to be one of the also-rans, I realised that he felt it would be impossible to emerge from Joey's shadow; in many respects, Joey's success and popularity was holding him back. Robert admitted to me in as many words that Joey was the King of Road Racing, that there would never be anyone quite like him and that there was no point in trying to be better than Joey because it would be impossible. By this stage, I was Robert's confidant and mentor, and I soon realised that I needed to speak up if he had the genuine desire to reach the top of his sport. I knew that I had a hell of a job on my hands to change his defeatist attitude and force him to get his priorities straight. It wasn't going to be easy: Robert had very little spare cash available, and a young wife and family to support. I knew that unless I acted quickly, Robert's career could be over before it even really started.

Rob and Joey were very different people. Joey was quiet, shunned publicity at every opportunity, and chose his friends and confidants carefully. Robert was much more outgoing and quite a cocky character, with a tendency to say the wrong things at the wrong time, which didn't endear him to some people. I admired Robert for saying what he felt was right, whether or not he was correct in his views; he was prepared to speak his mind and definitely wasn't someone who would say the things he knew other people wanted to hear. There were many who didn't wish us to succeed, wary of the possible threat posed by this young whippersnapper to their idol Joey. Others also attempted to drive a wedge between the two boys, but they were fools to even think that they could succeed on that front. Robert idolised Joey, and I know this for a fact.

There is one night that sticks in my mind, and that exemplifies the closeness of the boys' relationship. It was a Friday night, just before the North West 200. Robert and I had got his bikes fully prepared in my workshop. They had been cleaned to perfection and were sitting ready, in full racing mode for the next day. Normally the Friday nights before the North West were late nights when we burned the midnight oil. But this night we had everything ready in good time.

I advised Robert to take full advantage of our early finish by going to bed early for a change. But I should have known better

– Rob was always much too wound up with nerves to go to sleep early, and anyhow he always made a point of calling over to Joey's on his way home, just to have a chat and see how his preparations were going. Robert left my house at approximately 11.30 p.m. and after I'd had a wash and a cup of tea I went to bed at about midnight. But I always struggled to sleep well the night before a race and lots of things kept going through my mind – had we the bikes properly prepared, did we tighten every nut and bolt, did we check and then double-check, would it be dry or rainy, were the tyre pressures checked. It was a never-ending cycle of did we or didn't we.

I must have dozed off at some point, as I was woken by the sound of a vehicle in my yard at 1.30 a.m. I jumped out of bed and looked out of my bedroom window to see Joey's van turning and reversing towards my workshop door. I could see Joey at the wheel and Robert in the passenger seat. I quickly pulled on a pair of tracksuit bottoms and a jacket and went outside to see what was wrong.

Robert met me at my back door. 'Open up the workshop, LB,' he said. 'Joey's 125cc machine isn't revving out.' It transpired that Robert had called with Joey and had discovered that Joey was having problems with his machine. Rob had suggested that they bring it to my workshop to switch a few pieces from his own 125cc machine on a trial and error basis, in an attempt to pinpoint the defective component or part on Joey's bike.

So off came the fairing (the fibreglass bodywork) and we started by switching the exhaust pipes. No joy, so we tried the carburettors and then the ignition boxes. While all this was going on, I phoned a neighbour – also a Dunlop fan – to ask him to help me to block – illegally – both ends of our road from other traffic so that the boys could road test the bikes. It was surreal to watch Joey and Robert ride their bikes on a quiet country road in the pitch black and then swap the bikes, especially given that racing motorcycles have no lights. I will never forget that night, especially the moment when both brothers blasted past my front gate with their front wheels pawing the air, at speeds of over 100 mph. Dangerous, yes, but all in a day's work for these two world famous local gladiators, who just happened to be brothers.

It took a while but we finally found the problem – a faulty ignition on Joey's bike. Given that Robert and Joey were joint hot favourites to win the 125cc race, it was a testament to their relationship that Robert did everything he could to ensure that his biggest rival would have the same chance that he had on the day. Joey would have done the exact same for Robert – that was how they worked.

Not for the first time, we ended up putting Robert's bike back together in the early hours of the morning and then locking up the workshop as dawn was breaking. Bang went another of my supposed early nights before a big race.

I think that a lot of people assume that opportunities came Rob's way because of his surname but, in fact, it was very much the opposite. He was known as Joey's wee brother and the perception was that he would never be as successful, so what was the point in supporting him. The tired old expression decreed, 'He'll never be as good as Joey.' It wasn't our goal to try and emulate Joey: I firmly wanted Robert to become a star in his own right. I was determined that Robert would be given the platform to realise his own potential because I knew that he could become a very special rider.

Robert and I had some differences of opinion on how to move forward, and it took Rob a while to accept that my way was the right way. I drummed it into him that he would have to implement a major lifestyle change if he was to achieve his potential. Rob was extremely fortunate because he had managed to secure the backing of the best private sponsor I believe he ever had in PJ O'Kane, a haulage contractor from Garvagh in County Londonderry. Without question, PJ provided Rob with the right equipment in those early years that enabled him to become established and set him on his way to stardom – and he was firmly on my side when it came to Rob changing his lifestyle. I was also able to pass on some of my experience from my football days, which back then was a more professional sport than road racing.

We were embarking on a new adventure but with the deadly serious intention of going right to the very top and, with that in mind, meticulous machine preparation and Robert's total commitment to our objectives were of paramount importance. I needed to instil in Robert the absolute belief that he had what it took to win every race he entered, regardless of whether Joey was racing or not: brotherly love had to be set aside from when the green lights went out or the flag was raised until they crossed the finishing line. I made it clear to Robert that there was to be no love lost with Joey when they were on track together and Joey acknowledged this and accepted it himself. I know for a fact that Joey admired Robert even more when he started to put it up to him.

I insisted on total professionalism in every facet of the operation. We were a small, poor team in comparison to a lot of the other set-ups in the paddock, but I was more than content with a small inner circle because that way we could maintain those vital ingredients of trust and respect. We were thankful for PJ who, together with his wife Jean, provided Rob with as much financial support as they possibly could. And PJ offered much more than money, he added a touch of class to the project and became a highly respected figurehead; he always conducted himself in the proper manner and was firm but fair. He laid the foundations we needed to become a successful team. Robert soon began winning races on a frequent basis – a top class rider, a faithful sponsor and me as his right-hand man was proving a magical combination.

In 1989 PJ bought Rob a Honda RC30 Superbike and we

were able to get rid of that animal of a 250cc Yamaha, which had cost us a fortune to maintain. The RC30 was Honda's much-anticipated new machine but we had our fair share of problems with it while it was still in its infancy. It broke down at the North West 200 in its first year and, although the Honda technician, Ron Grant, argued that his recommended torque settings had not been adhered to, I personally believe he had made a blunder by giving us the wrong settings in the first place. The issues with the bike were eating into PJ's budget but he continued pumping in every penny he could in support of Rob's racing career. There was no doubt he had great affection for Robert and I often get the feeling that PJ saw him as the son he never had. That's not to say it was all plain sailing, though, because sometimes the relationship did become strained.

A major cause of tension was that Rob had a propensity for being badly organised, perhaps arriving for a race meeting only to find that he'd forgotten to pack the generator or the tyre warmers or the compressor, or that he hadn't completed the necessary paperwork for his race entry. I was still working as a plumber so most of the time it was Robert's responsibility to load up the van, and rarely did we turn up with everything that we needed for a race. This used to infuriate PJ. During the earlier years of Robert's career at a short circuit meeting at Kirkistown on the Ards Peninsula in County Down. Rob was riding a Honda RC30 at the meeting and the machine had been proving rather problematic in the lead-up to the race. Unsurprisingly, we experienced more engine issues that day at Kirkistown and were forced to strip it down. PJ had supplied Robert with a decent-sized tent to work in when we were preparing the bikes, but Robert had forgotten to bring the cover with him to Kirkistown. We only discovered this when we were erecting the frame of the tent and we had no choice but to get on with things in the open. As fate would have it, it began to rain and – of course – we were caught with no shelter and the engine of the RC30 lying in pieces. There were bike parts everywhere and to make matters worse, PJ arrived on the scene out of the blue with a friend. Rob had actually given up on having his own bike prepared in time and asked our great friend Joe Millar of Millar Transport, who was Eddie Laycock's sponsor, if we could borrow his RC30 Honda as Eddie was riding his 500cc Grand Prix machine instead. When PJ discovered this he was furious – not only was he deeply embarrassed by the unprofessionalism on show, with his engine lying in pieces on the ground inside a tent with no cover in full view of everyone, but to add insult to injury, Robert had borrowed a bike off a rival haulage contractor.

PJ exploded and ordered me to gather up all of the parts and put them in the race wagon and park the whole lot at his house. At the time, I felt that Robert was unaware of the serious implications of borrowing the bike from Joe Millar; he simply never stopped to think, and just wanted to be able to take part in the race. It seemed to me that this would be the end of PJ's sponsorship of Rob. I sincerely hoped that this wouldn't be the case, because I liked and respected PJ, and I knew that Robert did too. The relationship between the pair was strained for a good while afterwards, but as time passed, the tension eased, such was the respect they had for each other. The pair of them were so bloody stubborn that I very often had to use all my powers of diplomacy to keep the relationship on track.

It would be several more years before there was another blow-up – this time when PJ offered Robert's 125cc Honda to another rider when Robert was injured. Robert had still intended to compete at a big short circuit meeting at Aghadowey – an airfield circuit near Coleraine. Rob and I were busy preparing the Honda – the wee lady I called it – in my garage in Ballymoney when the news came through that PJ felt that Robert wouldn't be fit enough to do the bike justice. All hell broke loose and the phone line between the pair was red-hot – neither held back and the air turned blue. Robert disappeared for a couple of hours and I found out he'd gone to Joey's Bar in the town for a drink, which I didn't mind because I felt that he needed a cooling-off period. When I returned to the garage after my tea, a call came through from PJ. He was fuming: 'I won't take that kind of language from anyone, LB. He won't be on any of my bikes again.' I knew this time that there was a serious risk of a permanent split and when Robert returned to the garage later that night, I told him what PJ had said. Rob picked up a spanner and fired it across the garage, narrowly missing the wee bike. By nature, he could occasionally be short-tempered himself and now he was going into meltdown. I'd had enough and told him to wise up and lock up behind him because I was heading for home. The next morning when I arrived at the garage I found a note from Robert waiting for me, which simply read, 'Thanks for putting up with me LB.' I kept that wee note for years, but to my heartbreak I can no longer find it. Robert was never someone who was really able to say sorry, so that note was indicative of just how repentant he felt over the situation. The media had managed to get wind of the row between Robert and PJ and had their fill for a few days, but I had faith in my ability to bring the two of them back together because they adored each other. When the shit hit the fan between them, it did so spectacularly and the issue was always compounded because they were both so obstinate.

Four
A special victory

One of Robert's most memorable victories for PJ O'Kane came in the 1989 Grand Prix in Macau, an island and gambling haven located off the coast of Hong Kong. We'd been in 1988 when the race was famously won by 500cc Grand Prix star Kevin Schwantz on the Pepsi Suzuki. Rob rode well in the '88 race, so well we received a phone call to our room to say that American great Schwantz had requested our company down at the hotel swimming pool. We went down to see him and there he was, relaxing with his entourage. Schwantz was amazed that someone as small as Rob was able to race a 750cc Honda RC30 so well around a tight street circuit like Macau. He was a huge star, but a nice lad and he even opened his magnum of champagne and shared it around before we left for the prize-giving ceremony in another large hotel nearby. The Guia street circuit at Macau is incredibly dangerous, lined with Armco barriers and walls, and there isn't a protective safety bale in sight. But it suited Robert – whose experience at home was based on racing on public roads lined with trees, walls and hedges – so he knew exactly how to approach a circuit like Macau. He was desperately keen to win this race for one extra-special reason: virtually every other race Robert had won already had Joey's name on the trophy. Although Joey had tried previously, he hadn't won at Macau, and Robert, being immensely proud of the Dunlop name, wanted to see it inscribed on every trophy that he or Joey had ever raced for.

In 1989, he was given a superb opportunity to set the record straight – the unbeatable combination of Schwantz and his factory Grand Prix bike were absent from the line-up after the American's dominant win the previous year. We left no stone unturned in our preparation, as always. On race day, some light rain delayed the start twice – motorcycle racing only goes ahead at Macau if conditions are completely dry and slick tyres can be used as it is otherwise too dangerous. It was late afternoon by the time the race finally got underway and although it was dry, it was somewhat gloomy and the light was fading quite quickly. I recall the race director, Mike Trimby, telling me during the warm-up lap to warn Robert to be careful not to stray off the racing line as quite a few 'rollies' – small pieces of rubber – had been deposited on the track by the Formula 3 cars that had been on the circuit moments earlier. I passed the message on to Rob when he returned but his biggest concern was visibility due to the lack of light. I realised that he was wearing his preferred dark visor but we had no time to change to a clear alternative because the signal went out that the race was about to get underway. I gave Rob my usual message – only he and I will ever know what it was – and seconds later the lights flashed to green and the race was on. My heart was bursting through my chest because it was getting darker by the minute and that, combined with the fact that Macau was the second most dangerous circuit I had ever seen after the TT, left me sick with worry. I was nervous because I knew how much Robert wanted to win this race but I should never have doubted my man, who repelled really determined challenges by Phillip McCallen and experienced

German World Superbike rider Peter Rubatto to achieve a victory. Robert was ecstatic and I was so proud of him that day.

It was time for a celebration and the fun really began after the podium formalities. We were chauffeured back to the hotel and the prize-giving dinner and presentation wasn't due to take place until later that evening. But we faced a dilemma because Robert hadn't packed a suit for the lavish post-race dinner. The race was now on to furnish Rob with suitable attire. We secured the services of a rickshaw driver, who pedalled us downtown where we could take our pick of men's tailors. We made sure we got a driver with a good, strong-looking set of legs who could get there quickly because time was of the essence; he even ran a few red lights to help us out. In UK measurements, Rob was a size small, but – to his delight – a small in China was too tight even for him, so for once he would need a medium suit. I'll never forget him turning to me in the fitting room and saying, 'LB, I'm a bigger man than you ever thought.'

In no time at all, the lady with the sewing machine had a suit ready for Rob – he'd chosen a dark, pinstripe material – and he looked very smart for the big night ahead. Fabric in China is unbelievably cheap and Rob was able to have his suit tailor-made and purchase a silk shirt and tie, all for less than £60. The same rickshaw driver, whose legs had just about recovered from the initial journey, whisked us back to our hotel and I had a quick shower as Rob made a few phone calls back home to Louise, his mum and dad and PJ. We thought we were all set, but disaster struck when it transpired that there wasn't a clean pair of socks left for Rob. Any pairs we had were hanging up drying on a makeshift line in the bathroom. I offered to take mine off and give them to him but he was having none of it, pointing out that when he stood up, his trousers went right down to the top of his shoes and hid any bare skin. 'Problem solved, LB,' Rob said, 'nobody will know.' So off we went to the hotel lobby to meet up with the rest of the lads before travelling on to the gala presentation dinner. But rather than hailing a taxi, we decided it would be better fun if everyone went in a rickshaw so we could have a race to the awards venue. Once again we tried to find a driver with a good pair of legs and our luck was in, because we managed to hitch a ride with the very same guy who'd taken us downtown earlier. We did a deal on the price of the fare and then the race was well and truly on. Our man was quickly into his stride and took the lead but as we edged closer to our final destination another rickshaw gradually drew alongside us and suddenly we didn't feel quite so invincible. The other rickshaw was carrying Dubliner Eddie Laycock and his sponsor Joe Millar and, of course, they were laughing and cheering hysterically as they hauled themselves into the lead. There was nothing our man could do and we were pipped at the post by Eddie and Joe – the one and only time we lost in Macau that year. We were having dinner later when Eddie confessed that his driver had an incentive to go the extra mile: every time he began to tire, Joe was whipping out the Hong Kong dollars. No wonder the guy was pedalling as if his life depended on it!

After a fabulous meal, the awards ceremony was soon in full swing and amongst the guests that evening were Eddie Irvine and Martin Donnelly. Macau also hosts a Formula 3 and Touring Car race in addition to the motorcycle Grand Prix and there were many young prospects in the room that night who went on to great things. I was bursting with pride as I watched Rob stride up to the stage to collect his award, immaculate in his new tailor-made suit and beaming from ear to ear as he stood shoulder-to-shoulder with the rest of the winners. I was sitting right at the front of the room in a prime seat, along with Race Director Mike Trimby, his wife and the top Macau officials. Hordes of photographers jostled for space and the flashbulbs blazed repeatedly as the winners basked in the limelight. The next thing we knew, Rob and his fellow prize-winners were ushered to a row of seats that had been set up on the stage. It was at this exact moment that I realised that Robert's decision to brave the awards ceremony without a pair of socks had seriously backfired. As he took his seat, Rob's trouser legs were halfway up his shins and all you could see were two fully exposed bony ankles. The game was up, and a visibly shocked Mrs Trimby leaned over towards me and whispered in my ear, 'Liam, does Robert not have any socks on?' By this stage my face was like a baboon's arse and I shamefacedly shook my head as she looked at me incredulously. I honestly thought Mrs Trimby was close to fainting but her disbelief quickly gave way to a fit of laughing as Rob, meanwhile, smiled away uncomfortably on his seat up on the stage. As I explained the situation to her the rest of the table took a keen interest in the story and fell about laughing.

The following year we were attending the riders' briefing in our Macau hotel when Mike Trimby requested that Rob and I make our way to the front of the room, informing us that Mrs Trimby wished to make a special presentation. You've guessed it: she handed us each a brand new pack of socks and the place went into uproar. Mike loved working with Rob because he was a promoter's dream; firstly he was a Dunlop and a world-class road racer, plus he was a good speaker and he was a handsome fellow too. We all got on really well with one another and Mike even put us in charge of one of the Toyota minibuses allocated for the motorcycle competitors. It meant that we had the sole use of the bus once we had dropped the riders off at the hotel at the end of each day and we put it to good use, touring around the island of Macau. We went down to the shore and watched the native boat builders at work and I was amazed by their skills as they carved out the hulls with only primitive tools. The skyscrapers then were constructed using bamboo scaffolding tied together with rope and the height of some of the buildings assembled in this manner was mind-boggling. We took time out to visit the small settlements around the island, soaking up the unique culture – a million miles away from what we were used to back home.

Macau is an incredible place, but there were some aspects of the lifestyle that we were less enamoured by, not least the live animal restaurant we stumbled across in the backstreets. It was the first and only time I saw an owl in captivity. The windows were crammed full of live animals in cages and you simply picked what you fancied: a member of staff plucked it from its temporary residence, before returning a short time later with it cooked on a plate. Needless to say neither Rob nor myself fancied much on the menu. Indeed, Robert was an animal lover who adored all forms of wildlife and in the end I had to virtually drag him away after he lost his cool. A guy had arrived pushing a wheelbarrow with four little Labrador pups inside, alive and evidently up for sale to the highest bidder. A man who appeared to be the owner of the restaurant – for want of a better word – came outside and began to give the pups the once over. Robert had been upset before this unpleasant scene had unfolded, but now he was absolutely furious and he gave them both a mouthful, though I'm not entirely sure they understood what he was saying. Rob was going ballistic and I quickly stepped in to coax him away. Martial arts had never been a strong point of mine and I wanted to ensure we departed the scene safely.

There was another place we weren't keen on either, but for different reasons. Opposite the paddock, which was like a three-storey car park, there was a little canteen situated in the trees and it was the roughest, filthiest café I have ever come across in my life. The 'roof' was a mixture of wood, plastic bags and tin and had to be seen to be believed. The local municipal workers made up most of the clientele and I'll never forget the cook's method of testing the heat of the wok pan, which involved spitting into the pot to see if it sizzled and evaporated. It was stomach-churning and when I pointed it out to Eddie Laycock on his first visit, the look on his face was priceless. We only ever bought a tin of Coke there, but it became a favourite tourist attraction during our visits to Macau.

We always flew via Hong Kong and it was a sixteen-hour flight back then, with a dreaded landing at the end. The pilot basically had to fly his jumbo jet between the massive skyscrapers as he came in to land. You could actually make out the faces of people in the apartments as you came down and it was always a white-knuckle ride. One year I was sitting beside an English businessman who told me he had made the trip twice a year for the past fourteen years and that the final approach still left him terrified.

In those pre-9/11 days, when security was more relaxed, the pilots would sometimes invite passengers into the cockpit and this was a privilege that Rob and I were very fortunate to have. The control panel was ablaze with hundreds of lights and a mass of knobs and switches but the pilot was sitting nonchalantly chatting away to us with his back to the control panel. We were a bit nervous and, even though he explained that the plane was flying on auto-pilot, it was still difficult to relax completely. It was the middle of the night and I recall the pilot asking Rob if he shouldn't be sleeping, to which he replied, quick as a flash, 'Shouldn't you be looking where you're going?'

The machinery was stored in crates and flown out to Macau in advance of the main party of riders arriving on the island. The crates would be there in the paddock and we'd have to go along on the first day and take delivery of all the gear. We used to pack the tyres and tools, and Robert's leathers and helmet into the crate along with the bike; and then did the same at the end of the meeting – although the crates were shipped back, a journey that took two weeks. When Robert won the race in 1989 he was presented with a huge bottle of champagne, which must've been three feet high and twelve inches wide. He decided against opening it and instead came up with the idea that we'd pack it into the crate as a surprise for PJ when we arrived home.

The crate arrived safely back in Northern Ireland in due course and Robert began dismantling it, only to find that the bottle of champagne had vanished. How do you explain that one?

Perhaps the most bizarre memory I have of Macau was also in 1989 when Robert won the race for the first time. He had earned some good prize money and decided he would treat himself to a video camera. As part of the trip, we all stopped in Hong Kong for a week before returning home. With electrical goods on offer for a fraction of the price we would pay at home, Rob got a superb deal, but he was keen to stress to the shop owner that he didn't want to pay any duty when we arrived at customs. The guy told him to say that he had taken it with him on his trip. When we got to Heathrow, Robert – bold as brass – headed straight to the big green 'Nothing to Declare' exit and I did likewise. But as fate would have it, Rob was pulled aside by the customs officers as I walked straight through.

I waited for what seemed like an eternity out in Arrivals until former Kawasaki star Mick Grant told me that Robert had just been taken into the interrogation room. A short time later the late TT commentator Geoff Cannell came over to me and confirmed that Robert had been arrested. It was probably another three-quarters of an hour before a deflated-looking Robert finally came trudging through. He explained that the customs officials had asked where he'd bought the video camera and Rob stuck to his plan of telling them he had acquired it in the UK before he left for Macau. But, sadly for Robert, upon further inspection, the customs officers found the purchase receipt in the bottom of the camera bag. He was given the ultimatum of having the camera confiscated and returning to London at a later date to fight his case or stumping up a fine of £200 and paying the outstanding duty. He had no choice but to hold his hands up and pay the required amount, which used up the rest of his prize money. It turned out to be an expensive camera.

Another really funny moment that stands out from our travels to Macau occurred during the post-race week, which the entire travelling party always spent relaxing in Hong Kong. We were staying in a top city centre hotel but the only food that was complimentary was the breakfast, which could be obtained via a voucher that was pushed under our bedroom door early each morning. One day, we were surprised to find that the staff had slipped four vouchers into our room instead of the usual two. And so it was time for another of Robert's brainwaves: he suggested we keep the additional breakfast vouchers and use them to get a free dinner later in the hotel restaurant. That night, we dressed smartly and proceeded to the five-star eatery with our two breakfast coupons, and asked to see a couple of menus. We produced our vouchers and in seconds were surrounded by flustered waiters and staff saying 'breakfast, breakfast' in broken English. Robert stuck to the plan and in his broad north Antrim accent tried to convince them that the vouchers would work for dinner. The stand-off lasted for at least fifteen minutes but eventually we had to relent and, with our tails between our legs, we left the restaurant and headed out of the hotel into the city's dazzling neon lights to grab something to eat elsewhere. The news somehow got back to Mike Trimby and, at the next morning's riders' briefing, with everyone gathered together, he asked, 'Who were the two idiots trying to exchange two breakfast coupons for evening meals in the restaurant last night?' Everyone was looking at each other wondering who would try and pull such a stunt, and of course no one owned up, but I'm sure Mike knew exactly who it was because he gave us a wry smile later that day and we had many a laugh about it years later. I have so many fond recollections of Macau and it's a place I'd love to go back to again to retrace our footsteps and relive some of those wonderful memories. We took the racing extremely seriously as always but Rob and I certainly enjoyed the craic and he was an absolute star over there. His race-winning RC30

Honda resides in a museum in Macau to this very day, bearing testament to his achievements and serving as a fitting memory to Robert's legacy at the famous old race in China.

Five
A clean sweep

At the beginning of their association, PJ O'Kane supplied Robert with a van; in 1990 PJ purchased a decommissioned Ulsterbus, which he completely transformed into a bespoke motorhome with sleeping quarters including two bunk beds, a kitchen and lounge area, a toilet and shower and even a small workshop section at the rear. It was painted up in PJ's legendary green and white race colours and we really felt we'd arrived when it was finished.

We took the bus to every race meeting we went to at home and in England and even across Europe. We were the envy of the paddock in that thing. The radio was never off in it, and we shared a love of music, which was another of the many similarities between us. Rob's favourite album was UB40's Greatest Hits and although I wasn't a big fan initially, the more I heard those songs, the more they grew on me and now I love them: I even have the album installed in my jukebox at home. Each time I hear 'Rat in mi Kitchen' or 'Red Red Wine,' it transports me back to those days, some thirty years ago, when Robert's career was only beginning. The songs would be blaring out as we headed off on our travels and I can picture Rob rolling cigarettes from his wee pouch of tobacco while he steered with his feet. He became an expert at this unconventional mode of driving, even when he was at the wheel of the Ulsterbus. The steering was incredibly heavy and you'd have needed an extra portion of porridge in the morning before taking the wheel in that thing, but remarkably it mattered little to Rob, who threw his two legs up around the steering wheel when we reached a straight part of the road if he fancied a smoke and still managed to keep things in line. The looks on the faces of some drivers who drew alongside us on the M6 in England were priceless.

We shared the driving duties if we were away on a long trip, which usually worked well, but there was one narrow miss when we were returning home from a race at Donington Park. I usually drove the first part of the journey home to allow Rob to rest after his exertions on the bike, but Rob had asked to do the first shift this time. I climbed into the bunk as Rob took the wheel. I had barely been lying down for ten minutes when I felt the bus was being driven erratically which was especially noticeable because, by and large, Robert was a first-class driver. I made my way up to the front and to my horror I found Rob sound asleep at the wheel. I quickly took control and thankfully disaster was averted. It was the last time that Robert took the first driving shift after a race. It was a bloody close shave.

The British short circuit racing scene was extremely competitive in the nineties and all the Irish riders struggled against their English rivals. Many had inferior machinery and most ate and slept in the back of their vans in the racing paddocks; quite a few were partial to a beer or two the night before the race and perhaps weren't as focused as they needed to be. I think the sight of the big teams and riders with the latest machinery and massive motorhomes proved quite intimidating for the majority of riders from Ireland, and maybe they were beaten before they even went out on to the track. There was a known drinking culture amongst the Irish lads. In 1991, one evening at Cadwell Park in Lincolnshire, Alan Patterson, another competitor and good friend from Northern Ireland, came knocking on our van door. Alan and the lads wanted Robert and me to join them in the local bar for a few pints, but I had always made my rules and regulations clear to Rob and drinking on the eve of a race wasn't permitted. So I told Alan to count us out. Robert wasn't best pleased, of course, and although he said nothing, his behaviour for the remainder of that evening confirmed to me that he'd have loved to have gone for even one drink with his mates. The next day, though, Robert went out and won the 125cc race, so he could see that the policy was paying off and also that we were getting our priorities right.

Usually a punch-up is pretty much unheard of at a motorcycle race but on one particular occasion it was unavoidable. It was the Saturday before race day at Mallory Park and the weather was beautiful; the sun was shining and it was a real scorcher. The wee bike was stripped down and sitting on the bike bench and myself and Robert had our T-shirts off because of the heat. We worked hard all day, practically taking the bike apart and rebuilding it again ahead of Sunday's race. We got finished up around teatime and, after a bit of a freshen-up, Rob suggested we should go to the bar in the paddock for a game of pool. It was one of his favourite pastimes and he needed some cigarettes as well – he preferred to roll his own but he was out of tobacco. Being the evening before a race, we both ordered a large glass of orange juice and ice and made our way over to the pool table, placing our money on the side of the table to book our slot for a game. Robert was pretty good at pool and usually beat me but I still enjoyed a game, and playing was a good way to unwind during a race weekend. We were about halfway through our game when I became conscious of three English lads who were in the bar. It was clear they'd had a few too many and soon they approached the pool table, carrying plastic pint glasses of beer. At first they stood and watched, but soon they started to mouth off. The biggest one opened with a sarcastic comment, saying, 'Oh look, it's Robbie Dunlop. My God he's small, his mum wouldn't have been very fat when she was carrying him.' As I made to react Robert muttered to me to leave it: he knew I had zero tolerance when it came to rudeness and bad manners and this guy was a prime example. We both played on and attempted to ignore them but the big guy was intent on starting trouble and as I went to play my shot, he blurted out, 'Foul shot, you touched the white first.' My patience had run out. I made towards him and before he could say boo, I slammed my fist into his stomach. As he slumped to the floor, I planted my left fist into the second guy's head, square on his dial, and he disappeared through a stud partition, landing flat on his back. At this point Rob had the smallest of the trio pinned in the corner of the pool room, holding the cue above his head by the narrow end and using it like a club. It honestly resembled a scene from the Wild West. A couple of huge guys wearing dickie bows and white shirts barged in and I thought things were going to get even more exciting, but they actually apologised to us and said they'd already had words with the three louts about their behaviour before we arrived. The bouncers scooped the first two off the floor and escorted all three off the premises. There was beer everywhere and the stud partition wall was quite badly damaged, but I must commend the proprietors: they too apologised for our troubles and offered us a meal each on the house. With the drama over, we managed to complete our game of pool in peace as the staff cleaned up the mess around us.

Robert had been wiping the floor with the opposition in 1991 and it got to the stage where the organisers attempted to lure back some of the big name riders from the Grand Prix scene, which I believe was an effort to halt his winning streak. Grand Prix rider Alex Bedford had entered for the round at Mallory Park. Most people I spoke to were of the opinion that he had probably been enticed to come and race to put a stop to Robert's dominance of the class. I think there were some people who didn't like the idea that that the British title might be taken out of England. Everyone was talking about this special appearance by the mighty Bedford, but it made no difference to Robert and me. We just went about our business in the same meticulous manner as always and left no stone unturned in our preparation. We had the wee lady sitting ready for scrutineering the night before the race; she was mint and ready to go. We both had a shower and got changed. Robert cooked the dinner, which was always spuds with something, and I did the washing up. We went for our normal pre-race walk around the track afterwards, checking every bump and hollow, and pinpointing the grippy parts of the circuit and the slippery parts. Once we were satisfied, we headed back to the van and turned in for the night at around eleven o'clock.

Around an hour later, Rob whispered, 'Are you sleeping LB?' to which I replied, 'Of course not. Why?' 'I think we've got the internal gear ratios wrong,' Robert explained. 'I think they could be better.' Robert had been lying there wracking his brains over the set-up of the bike for the race and felt he could gain up to half a second a lap with the changes he had in mind. In those days, changing the internal gearbox ratios meant taking the engine out of the bike and stripping it right down. The whole gear ratio also had to be restructured: it wasn't a matter of one simple change. It was a big job but, typically, Robert didn't want to leave anything to chance, even if he knew we were going to have to work through the night to make the necessary alterations. We dragged ourselves out of bed and began a complete strip down of the wee lady. I remember that daylight had broken and the sun was beginning to rise by the time we had finished.

I managed to grab a few hours' kip before it was time to take the bike down to scrutineering. I left Robert asleep so that he got as much rest as possible for the race. When I came back I made some tea and toast before I woke Rob, probably around about forty minutes before the first morning warm-up practice session. He liked his kip and didn't want to be woken up any earlier than was absolutely necessary on a race morning. We had a bit of a ritual that we went through at each race: I would warm up his leathers and gloves by the heater in the van because Robert felt that a set of leathers were always a much better fit when they had been heated. He wouldn't have been the most talkative person first thing in the morning, like a lot of people when they crawl out of their scratcher, and I knew when to talk and when to shut up. I was probably as stoked up with adrenaline as Robert was, but I always ensured I acted calmly and presented a cool front.

Soon it was time to make our way to the warm-up area for the race and the first thing we noticed was the size of the crowd. A lot of people had turned up, no doubt keen to see the big star, Alex Bedford, in action. The weather was fine and the grid for the 125cc race was crammed with potential winners, all quality pilots; many with Grand Prix experience and riding trick machinery. I knew that our bike wasn't the most expensive thing on the grid, but no stone had been left unturned in its preparation, especially on the internal gear selection. The grid formed up and the riders, including Rob, Bedford, Steve Patrickson and Rob Orme, fixed their steely gaze on the lights. Britain's best were out to put an end to Robert's winning run and had the partisan support of the massive crowd urging them on. The scene was set and, once the lights changed to green, the air was filled with the unmistakable noise of screaming two-strokes at full revs, charging down to the first corner like a swarm of angry bees. Our tactics turned out to be bang on the money and Rob obliterated the other riders. He rode like the champion he was soon to become, stretching away to win by six seconds from Bedford after twelve laps – a winning margin of victory that represented an advantage of half a second per lap, precisely what Rob had predicted he could gain if we made those changes to the internal gear selections. We took great satisfaction from that particular victory, not only because Rob maintained his unbroken winning streak, but also because he had shown a clear pair of heels to Bedford. Many people thought the Grand Prix star would clean up, but Rob showed them how good he really was.

All week the English fans had been proudly walking around wearing their specially printed Alex Bedford T-shirts, which I remember were emblazoned with the warning 'Bedford Is Back!' across the front. As I wheeled our wee lady into the winners' enclosure, I noticed Bedford's team were all there in parc fermé, the area where the winning three riders and their teams gather immediately after a race. To say they didn't appear overly pleased that their man had been forced to play second fiddle to Rob is an understatement – the Grand Prix rider had been well and truly stuffed in his own back yard and I could tell by the looks on their faces that they were thinking, 'This guy Dunlop really is as good as they say.' I couldn't resist rubbing it in, so I went over and shook their hands, saying, 'Hard luck, lads, but don't dump the T-shirts –maybe you could add the word "well" so that it reads "Bedford Is Well Back".' They were fuming and the fact that Rob was in fits of laughter didn't help matters. Maybe I should have resisted the temptation to wind them up, but for three days before the race their heads had been too far up their own arses to even consider Rob a threat. This wee guy called Dunlop from little Northern Ireland was special and they now knew this in no uncertain terms.

After a quick bite to eat, we set off on our journey back to the Toon (Ballymoney) with the winners' laurel wreath hanging on the door mirror of the passenger side. I was driving and Rob made sure I did a full lap of the paddock before we left. We were showing off a bit but it was also a psychological move, a show of strength to put down a marker for the next round: we'd be back and we were letting them all know it.

Robert was using Bridgestone tyres to great effect in 1991 and, given his success, the company was experiencing record sales. Any merchandise that Rob was promoting was also flying off the shelves. It really was a very special time in his career: Robert was becoming a star, even if he didn't quite realise it at that point. He may have been dominating every round in the British Championship but the financial reward for his achievements was nothing spectacular. Travel costs were high as we were sailing across the Irish Sea to compete in England almost every two weeks and we had to keep ourselves for three or four days at a time at each round. We tried to keep the costs down as much as we could, so spuds and beans were the staple diet, plus I must admit that we weren't averse to filling up the van from the red diesel pump. By this time, Robert had signed for the factory Norton team. It was a dream come true for him and our dear friend Barry Symmons, who had previously been Joey's boss in the works Honda Britain team, was instrumental in making it happen. Barry was the team manager for Norton and was prepared to take a chance on Rob at a time when other factory squads weren't. It was a shrewd move on Barry's behalf. He was very good to us, and his dear wife Lorna would regularly bring us over some toast and marmalade in the mornings. I think they knew the larder in our van was usually bare. Before I knew Barry properly, I thought of him as a rather dour sergeant major-type figure but I couldn't have been more wrong. Barry was the consummate gentleman and was always very kind to the pair of us — many a night he put us up in his house in Lichfield in Staffordshire and never expected a penny in return.

One visit was especially memorable. We had spent the Friday night at Barry's house and the following day we wanted to gain access to the Norton factory to use one of the lathe machines to carry out some modifications to a rear wheel spacer for the bike. The factory was closed until lunchtime, so we decided to take a walk through the town centre to do a spot of sightseeing. It was a lovely sunny morning and we wandered around the quaint cobbled streets at our leisure. We eventually spotted a sign advertising an antiques sale. We decided to pop in and have a look around, so we made our way up the broad staircase to the first floor and sure enough there was a large display of some rather fine antiques of all shapes and sizes. It spanned a very large area and several members of staff were dotted around. Not many customers had arrived yet and Robert and I went our separate ways, walking around looking at the various pieces until something took our fancy. Rob liked antiques and spent quite some time looking through a large and varied collection of old books.

Meanwhile, I was in an area where a set of china was on display and, typically, it was here that disaster struck. I had innocently picked up a lovely old butter dish but, as I turned it upside down to look for the price, to my horror the lid fell off and shattered on the floor. There had been an almighty crash as the lid smashed into a hundred pieces and I was mortified as I stood there looking down at the floor. In a flash, various members of staff had surrounded me and started chittering like hens in a deep litter house. I felt as though I was in an echo chamber as the exclamation that I had 'broken it' appeared to go on forever. Then, to my amazement, I heard an unmistakeable north Antrim voice in the midst of all these exasperated English ladies, which chipped in, 'Aw aye, ye hae broken it.' Of course it was Rob, who couldn't resist the chance to join the commotion. It wasn't enough for him that I was getting it from every angle from the staff, but he had to stick the boot in as well. He was grinning from ear to ear, but the situation was about to take a turn for the worse. On closer inspection, it was discovered that, not only had the lid of the antique butter dish been broken, but it had dropped on to another plate and smashed that as well. Eventually one lady, who was wearing a pair of glasses with a chain, delivered the body blow I had been expecting: 'I expect you have read all the signs up here, sir. If you break it, you pay for it.' I muttered a lame excuse that the dish and lid should have been taped together with Sellotape or the like, but she was having none of it. Cue Robert, who piped in again, 'Oh yes, sir, the signs are all clearly displayed, you'll have to pay for both pieces in full.' He was clearly loving every minute of it but I continued to plead my case. To my amazement one of ladies – the youngest-looking one – spoke up and declared that she agreed with me that the pieces should have been taped together, particularly given that the price was on the underside of the butter dish. The beads of sweat that had been lashing off my forehead began to lessen ever so slightly and I could see the slightest glimmer of light at the end of the tunnel. Whilst one of the ladies tallied up the cost of the broken items, which came to £120, they told me to give them a few minutes while they held a quick meeting to decide my fate. I agreed, although it seemed like a kangaroo court to me.

By this stage, Robert and I had realised that we probably didn't have the £120 between us. As the group of ladies debated their final decision, we became aware that some kind of band was passing by on the street outside. Rob took one look at me and said, 'LB, do you see that big staircase we came up? Well, ease yourself over to the top of it because we're getting out of here.' As nonchalantly as we could, we edged our way over to the giant staircase and once we arrived, with about four giant leaps each we bundled out into the street and straight into the middle of a morris dancers' parade. The troupe had unexpectedly acquired two new members and we enthusiastically kicked our heels up and joined in with the knee lifts as we left the antiques sale disaster behind. I can still picture Rob to this day laughing his head off as he danced away with the parade.

When we finally made it to the Norton factory, our boss and host Barry Symmons was already there and, being a shrewd man, he quickly sussed that we had been up to some kind of mischief. We spilled the beans and Barry wasn't best pleased, telling us that we should have waited for the final verdict instead of taking off. And of course he was right. After we had manufactured the rear wheel spacer for the bike at the factory, Rob and I went to have a look at the very old local church, which was still in use and still had cannonball dents in the outside walls, apparently from the Cromwell era. Rob loved learning the history of old buildings and he was in his element as we explored that church and read up on its past. In the meantime, Barry – being the man that he is – had gone to the antique fair to check if there was any outstanding bill to pay. Thankfully, it transpired that there wasn't, although the ladies there did ask him if we had nipped out for a bite of lunch while they were deliberating. Needless to say that these days, if I'm ever anywhere near an antique, I keep my hands firmly in my pockets.

The Haslam family also became good friends and Ron and his wife Anne frequently sent for us to come over to their big motorhome for a cooked dinner; a real luxury for Rob and me in those British championship days. We were also grateful to Fred Clarke, the commentator whose voice is immediately recognisable to anyone who has been to a British Championship race over the past thirty-five years. Fred always checked up on us at every race, popping in to say hello and making sure we were all right. We received a warm welcome from a handful of others but, by and large, the biggest majority of people in the paddock couldn't see us far enough. Robert Dunlop, the little Ulsterman, was a class apart – a superior force at every circuit and some organisers and fans didn't like it one bit. He'd been winning races and setting lap records galore and people were desperate to know what the secret of our success was. Some reckoned it was the Bridgestone YCX tyres, others felt it was the fuel we were using or our suspension set-up, but they were all wrong: the difference was Robert. It wasn't what was in the bike, it was the man on it. Rob was in a league of his own that year – he was world class.

One night that year we had worked later at the bike than normal and rather than walk the circuit as we normally did to check out the condition of the track, we adopted a different approach after an opportunity presented itself that was too good to turn down. It was at Oulton Park and Robert had spied two mountain bikes resting against the side of a motorhome. We decided to borrow them to lap the circuit and off we went on our way. We were pedalling like the clappers along the start and finish straight when suddenly in the gloom ahead we spotted that some crash barriers had been placed across the start and finish to prevent anyone from driving around the circuit. Rob shouted, 'It's okay, LB, there's a two-foot gap between each one.' We were really flying at this point so we each picked a gap and went for it, but at the very last second I noticed a chain link stretching across from barrier to barrier and before we could do anything about it, we were launched over the handlebars, landing some way up the track. I thought we were goners but then, after a moment or two, I heard Rob moaning and I realised I was still conscious. 'Are you okay?' I asked him, to which came the response, 'Not bad.' Once I saw he was able to get on to his feet then my fears about the race the next day were allayed. Battered and bruised, we left the mountain bikes back, although not quite in the condition we had found them, it has to be said. We crawled into our bunks to lick our wounds. Although Robert was feeling a bit stiff and sore the following morning, he went out and did the business on track and no one was any the wiser about the night before.

We were living by the seat of our pants in those days but it was a barrel of laughs. During that same great '91 season we stayed at Carl Fogarty's house for the Brands Hatch round. We had managed to get another rider to take our bikes and equipment over so, for once, Rob and I flew and were picked up at the airport by Carl's wife, Michaela. We stayed with the Fogartys for three days, commuting back and forth from their house to the track. It was damp and rainy for practice, conditions Rob never liked, so he was quite well down the field. The next morning we were working at the bike in the paddock when this young, aspiring journalist from a well-known motorcycle magazine approached Rob with a notebook and pen in hand and asked if there was any chance he could get a word with Rob. The guy looked nervous and seemed a bit wet behind the ears, but Rob agreed. The young reporter remarked that it hadn't been a great practice session and asked if the wet conditions had been a factor, adding, 'You didn't look yourself out there.' Robert beckoned the lad over and whispered, 'Can I let you into a secret?' The young guy was nodding his head, clearly excited at the prospect of getting an exclusive. Robert continued, 'You're 100 per cent right. It wasn't me out there on the bike, it was LB.' 'My God, I just knew that wasn't the shape of you out there', the reporter replied. 'Does that happen much? Does LB do many of the practice sessions?' With a look of mischief on his face, Robert replied, 'Only when it's wet – I hate the wet so I always send LB out there to qualify in the rain.'

The young guy was flabbergasted and Robert knew he had him hook, line and sinker. Keen to know more, he asked, 'Does LB have any bother getting into your leathers and helmet?' Without a moment's hesitation, Rob said, 'The leathers are a bit tight and sometimes it's hard to get the helmet off LB's head.' The lad was shaking his head in disbelief and before he walked off he reassured us: 'Don't worry, your secret is safe with me.' It was all we could do to compose ourselves but the biggest laugh of all was yet to come. On the morning of the final practice session, all the riders were sitting in the warm-up area, waiting for the gate to open to allow them to proceed on to the circuit. I had left Robert on his own but, when I looked back, I spotted the young journalist getting up close to Rob, peering into the dark tinted visor he was wearing. He then knocked the side of Robert's helmet with a knuckle and I saw him mouth a few words. Later that evening I remembered to ask Robert what he had said and Rob began to break into a fit of laughter as he told me, 'He tapped my helmet LB and said "Is that you Robert?"' We were in stitches and we often wondered how many times that young journalist would have recounted the story to disbelieving fans or his mates in the pub, insisting that when it was wet, I went out and qualified the bike!

Robert went on to wrap up the British Shell Oils title by a commanding margin. In my eyes he finished the season unbeaten and won every single race, even if there was huge controversy at Donington Park. Robert had been battling with Rob Orme and at the final bend on the very last lap at Goddard's Orme wiped Rob out from behind and the pair went sprawling. Orme had attempted an impossible move and Robert sustained a broken collarbone in the incident along with cracked ribs, but nonetheless he quickly remounted and crossed the finishing line in first position. He was immediately taken to the medical centre at the circuit to have his collarbone plated and in the meantime I went looking for Orme. I was absolutely furious and, as I stormed off in search of him, Norton's Barry Symmons was running after me trying to get me to calm down. I was having none of it: in my eyes Orme was nothing more than a bitter loser who couldn't accept that an Ulsterman was coming over to England every weekend and beating him on his own soil. Orme was a cocky so-and-so but on this occasion he was running scared. His mechanic told me he had disappeared, but I later heard he was hiding in a cupboard in someone else's motorhome. It was probably a good decision on his behalf, because if I'd laid my hands on him I'd have nailed him good and proper.

Robert was later disqualified from the result at Donington by the organisers, who reinforced the rule that the rider had completely parted company from his machine and therefore should not have remounted and returned to the track. English glamour boy Orme finished third in the championship without winning a single race, but all the glory belonged to Rob. Amazingly, Rob went to the Isle of Man TT a week later and won the 125cc race with his collarbone still plated, which exemplifies the kind of hard-as-nails sportsman he was. Just three years ago, the ambition of becoming a British champion had seemed a pipe dream, but Robert had grown in stature from someone lacking drive and confidence to a rider who was making his mark in the road racing world. His CV now made impressive reading and I was very proud of what he had accomplished. Rob had kept his word to me and I had fulfilled my end of the bargain; we were indeed a formidable combination.

Six

Ups and downs

Robert's performance to beat Alex Bedford is an abiding memory of mine, but another race on the short circuits that really showcased Robert at his best was in 1993, at a European Championship meeting held at Kirkistown in County Down, which hosted a round of the series for several years in the early nineties. We were granted an entry for the race and, even though we knew the field would include riders who had the potential to go on and become future world champions, we were quietly confident we could give them a run for their money if the wee lady was set up to perfection. On the day prior to the race we went for a walk through the paddock and we certainly had our eyes opened: each of the top European riders had at least two bikes in each awning; some even had three machines at their disposal. It was a massive advantage because it meant that they could have a bike sitting prepared and ready to suit whatever weather conditions might materialise. They wouldn't find themselves standing on the start line with a wet tyre in one hand, an intermediate in the other and a slick between their legs half an hour before the race was due to start if the weather was uncertain – always a distinct possibility at Kirkistown.

The presence of all these tanned Europeans with their slick, professional set-ups only served to strengthen Robert's resolve. We kept our own counsel and, on the eve of the race, tucked into a big barbecue cooked up for us by our good friends Alex and Bertie from Portrush, who were always on hand with the grub any time we went to Kirkistown. We bedded down in the back of the van and, to my delight, race morning dawned bright and dry.

I knew that with all the media attention focused on the big European stars we could get on with our own preparations quietly, and that suited us fine, allowing Robert to slip under the radar. The grid was crammed full of top European contenders in all their finery but once the lights went out, Rob quickly showed that he was a match for any of them. He oozed class that day from the word go and soon had their measure. They never really saw which way he went and Rob simply left a world-class field in his wake, going on to win the race by almost half-a-lap. It was a dazzling performance and Billy Nutt told me afterwards that it was one of the best displays he had ever witnessed by a rider from Northern Ireland. I was keeping my fingers crossed that this particular result, coupled with Rob's all-conquering British title success in 1991, would help us attract a big name sponsor to go Grand Prix racing. Unfortunately, nothing ever came of that hope. I always regret that Rob was never granted that opportunity because I am absolutely positive that he had the ability to be successful at world championship level. A few years later I watched those same riders who had been obliterated by Robert at Kirkistown excelling in Grand Prix competition and I did so with a heavy heart, because my enduring feeling was 'if only'.

Robert took the chance to ride in selected 125cc European rounds when they came up and one particularly unwelcome memory springs to mind one year when we went to Monza. By this time we had gone up in the world and were travelling in a nice motorhome supplied by a sponsor called John Kennedy from Garvagh. I never had a lot of time for John but ultimately Robert was benefitting from his backing and that was really all that mattered. We set off from Ballymoney having planned our route to take in the shortest ferry crossing possible, as usual. We drove from Stranraer to Dover then sailed to Calais and continued on through France, Belgium, Germany and Switzerland before finally arriving in Italy. Once we reached Germany we stayed overnight at the home of a top technician who worked for Honda, who lived in a beautiful log cabin near the city of Nuremberg, close to the circuit of Nürburgring. He advised us to visit an extinct volcano nearby that had become a magnificent lake and what an experience that turned out to be. Rob and myself rose early the next morning and made our way to the lake, crossing the water over a wooden walkway before taking our shoes off and dangling our feet in the lukewarm water. Occasionally the odd bubble would have risen to the surface, not dissimilar to a fart in the bath. Not only was it a privilege to see a place of such incredible beauty, but our feet also made contact with water for the first time in over a week and so conditions were altogether more pleasant in the motorhome for the remainder of the trip. The scenery in Switzerland was breathtaking, with little chalets nestled at the edge of picturesque lakes in the shadow of the majestic Swiss Alps. I can picture the reflection of the lights from those chalets shimmering over the surface of the water as dusk began to fall and it was such a spectacle that neither of us was in a rush to have a kip. We were only two lads from the Toon and it wasn't every day that we got to marvel at such a spectacle, so we were loath to turn in for fear of missing something.

We arrived at the Monza circuit and drove into the complex agog: it was a spectacular place and a completely different world to anything we'd experienced before. As comparative unknowns we were directed into a paddock where competitors of a supposed similar standing were accommodated, which put my back up straight away.

Exhausted, we bedded down and were awakened the next morning by the sound of torrential rain battering the roof of the motorhome. It was lashing down as Robert went out in the first practice session. I made my way to the pit lane, where I remember standing watching beside Italian star Loris Capirossi, the former 125cc and 250cc world champion and multiple 500cc Grand Prix race winner. Robert qualified poorly in the wet and was finding it difficult to adapt to the width of the circuit. He improved his time in the second session later that evening but was still only in the middle of the grid in terms of his lap speed. Granted, he was up against the best in Europe but Rob knew he was capable of going much faster and we both expected better.

The rain was still incessant the next morning and, following Robert's warm-up session, I knew that he still wasn't properly dialled in. I dried his leathers, boots and gloves by the heater when he came back in and, as the rain continued to hammer down outside, I instinctively knew that Robert wouldn't be at his best during the race. The wet track was making things difficult and Robert wasn't particularly fond of the place either. He would have to start from halfway down the grid and, in the wet conditions, it would be impossible for him to make any decent headway, not least because of the spray that would be kicked up by the riders ahead of him. In hindsight, I wish I had suggested that we call it a day and head for home.

The call came for the riders to assemble in the warm-up area and I told Robert I'd gather up some tools and meet him out on the grid. As I made my way to the pit lane I could hear the bikes out on their warm-up lap and once I was nearer to the track I could see a red flag being waved. Initially I thought it was merely to bring the riders to a halt on the grid after they'd completed their lap, but as I gazed up towards the infamous final corner at Monza – the Parabolica – to try and pick Robert out in the gloom, a rider who was staying in the same paddock told me that Robert had fallen off. I remember saying, 'Sorry, you've made a mistake, mate. My rider would never fall off on a warm-up lap.' He shrugged his shoulders and toured further up the pit lane. One by one the competitors streamed past and then another rider stopped and told me the same thing. I still thought they must have got it wrong but then I saw the recovery truck with our wee lady in the back. I was absolutely stunned. Rob had never fallen off on the warm-up lap.

My immediate concern was for Rob's welfare and I made my way to the large medical centre, where Rob was treated by Dr Claudio Costa, the famous Grand Prix doctor who established the legendary Clinica Mobile, which has been an ever-present sight at world championship race meetings now for more than thirty years. I was asked to take a seat in reception. Almost straight away I could hear Robert shouting in pain and I tried to make my way to the theatre area where I thought he was, but I was stopped. Before too long I was ushered to the rear exit of the building where Robert was in the process of being lifted into the back of an ambulance. He spied me and shouted, 'Tell them to go easy, LB. I'm in agony here.' The words had no sooner left his mouth than they banged the stretcher against the rear of the ambulance as they were lifting him in. Rob let out one almighty scream.

I was told that his injuries were all pelvis-related. That was a huge relief – broken bones usually heal in time, but head and spinal injuries are the biggest danger to a rider. It was a bit of a taboo subject, but we all knew the potential implications of a bad head injury. Robert was always very particular over the type of head protection he wore. He had great faith in the Arai brand throughout his career, which was also the choice of his older brother Joey. With Rob en route to hospital, I made my way back to the paddock to collect the damaged bike and pack everything away. Around three hours later I pulled out of the paddock and headed to the hospital in the motorhome. Driving around Milan is quite an experience, I can tell you. It was total gridlock with cars blasting their horns and jostling for position, and it felt like quite an achievement when I finally pulled into the hospital car park without a scratch on the motorhome or trailer. I gathered up some baggy clothes for Rob, put some food into a bag and went to find him. He was up on the sixth floor but when I got there I was told to come back in another two hours as the doctors were still working on him. I was absolutely shattered and lay down for a few hours' kip after having something to eat in the motorhome. I managed to see Robert later that night and he was lying there bandaged up like a mummy and heavily sedated.

The next morning Robert was awake and bright as a button when I went to visit him. His injuries included severe dislocations and fractures, particularly around the area of his pelvis. I asked him what the hell had happened and warned him never to talk to me again about idiots who fell off on a warm-up lap. We both had a chuckle at that and Robert explained that he had lost the front end on a fast right-hander around the back of the circuit. The belly pans of the Formula 1 cars had been grinding against the surface; coupled with the torrential rain, the corner had been left like an ice rink. Robert was catapulted into the straw bales at the side of the track when he came off and because they had been saturated by rain then he might as well have slid into solid rocks. Rob told me that I should head on home as they were talking about flying him back in an air ambulance. I wasn't very keen on leaving him behind – I'd never done it before and I didn't want to do it now. However, I tracked down the doctor and he explained to me that Robert was likely to be in hospital for around two weeks and that it would indeed be necessary to fly him home in an air ambulance. The doctor told me to leave some clothes for Rob and to take most of his other personal effects home with me, so I opened a wardrobe door in the ward and began to fire all the clothes he wouldn't need into a big yellow bag. It was then that this wee man who was lying prostrate next to Robert and bandaged up to the neck began flailing his arms and legs around, with the traction cables and weights flying everywhere. I shouted, 'Nurse, nurse, come quickly this man's having a fit or something.' The doctor rushed to his side as well and after a very brief discussion was able to inform me that I was in fact putting that patient's possessions into a bag, rather than Rob's. I erupted into fits of laughter and so did Robert, who was shouting at me, 'Stop it, stop it, LB. I can't take any more.' It helped to lift our mood a bit.

It was with a heavy heart that I said farewell to Rob. I'd never left him behind so far from home in my entire life but I'd been in touch with his wife, Louise, who told me it would be pointless to remain there with him for the next fortnight. I set off on my journey home and, with the exception of fuel stops and the ferry crossings, I never pulled in once for a rest. When I got to Ballymoney I almost fell out of the driver's seat I was so exhausted. Robert was flown back to Northern Ireland via air ambulance and spent some time undergoing rehabilitation work at the Ulster Hospital in Dundonald, where the staff have always been magnificent.

Seven
The glory days

Robert had his own ideas and thoughts with regards to eating habits. He detested microwave ovens and in particular anything cooked or heated in them – at that time, they were fairly new, and he wasn't totally convinced that they were safe. I can remember the two of us arriving at our accommodation in the south of Ireland one time when he was down to compete at the now defunct Fore Road Races. The people we were staying with were extremely nice and the lady of the house had cooked us a beautiful steak dinner in preparation for our arrival. We arrived about one hour late – both of us were starving and the lady sat us down at the kitchen table and proceeded to heat our two dinners in the microwave. I immediately got stuck into mine but Rob declined to eat his and told the dumbstruck lady why. The problem was solved when the lady kindly rustled him up a chicken salad and it was forgotten about. I wasn't best pleased and told Rob afterwards that I had taken exception to his refusal to eat his dinner.

That particular race meeting proved to be a successful one in a rather unique way. Robert, who was carrying the number four, managed to win four races at an event called Fore, so it's one that always sticks out in my mind. I can remember us going up to the main pub in the square after the races; it was always packed. We quickly agreed to rearrange our plans for an immediate return home and instead decided to stay there for a few pints, opting to return home the following day. Quite a few fans from Ballymoney often went to Fore and we met up with them and joined in the party. I always wished that we could bottle that genuine feel-good factor of cross-community goodwill, which existed amongst all road racing fans across the entire island. Never once did I detect any sectarianism despite major differences at government level between north and south. The motorcycle family were as one, proof yet again that sport is a great common denominator and continues to break down political barriers and build the kind of bridges that politicians simply cannot.

Robert competed at the majority of road races in the south of Ireland but I particularly liked the Skerries meeting. He was also a fairly frequent competitor at Mondello Park but I never felt it suited Robert and I don't believe he performed at his best there. It was on a journey home from Mondello Park that I almost killed us both. I was driving our van and Robert was sound asleep in the passenger seat. We were nearly home and it was dark when I went into a right-hand downhill bend much too fast and, as I did so, the bend got tighter. The bend was lined with trees and as I tried desperately to steer my way through, the van began to tip on to its two outside wheels until it was on the point of tipping over at about 80mph. Miraculously, the van returned to its four wheels, doing so with a bang, which resulted in us swerving all the way through the seemingly never-ending bend. By this stage Robert was wide awake and quietly said, 'We'll never be as close to death as that again, LB.'

I still use that same road and that downhill right-hand band sends shivers up my spine. It was also on a return journey from

Mondello Park when, completely out of the blue, Robert made a comment which almost caused me to drive straight through the large Dunsilly roundabout outside Antrim. Rob had been quiet for about an hour so I thought he was sleeping but later, like a bolt out of the blue, Rob said, 'If anything should ever happen me, LB, I'd like you to organise a memorial trophy incorporating my helmet design.' He also said he'd like his wife Louise to keep his wedding ring. In spite of all our years together and the fact that we always discussed everything: racing, family and private matters, we'd never discussed the possibility of his death. So his unexpected request completely took me by surprise. I was so taken aback that I actually told him to be quiet, that I never wanted to contemplate such a scenario. I was still concerned by Robert's train of thought because this was the one and only time when he ever tried to raise the subject. Even when we attended the funerals of other riders killed in the sport, we never really debated what had happened or why they had crashed – it was taboo. Robert was genuinely affected by sorrow on these occasions, but as soon as the funeral was over, it was business as usual again and the preparations for the next race began.

In motorcycle road racing, three meetings are of the utmost importance: the North West 200, the Isle of Man TT and the Ulster Grand Prix, the three majors as I call them. Rob and I always geared our preparations around these and, while it was all well and good picking up wins at the smaller national road races, the three majors offered greater financial rewards as well as the opportunity to tick more important boxes on your CV. It was at these races that the Dunlops really excelled. Not only could they win at the bread and butter events, but they also had a God-given talent and ability that enabled them to take their racing to the next level at the main international meetings. When the best riders in the world were in town, you could always count on a Dunlop to take the fight to them.

The Ulster Grand Prix at the legendary Dundrod circuit above the hills near Belfast was always one of Robert's favourite courses, and will always hold a special place in my heart. I'm grateful for the memories I shared there with Robert and the team. Dundrod today holds the honour of being the fastest road race in the world with New Zealand's Bruce Anstey setting the outright lap record of 133.977mph in 2010. The course is steeped in history and has remained largely unchanged since it was first used in 1953. Its fast and flowing nature and the absence of man-made chicanes make it the favourite road race for most of the sport's biggest names.

An iconic race meeting in Northern Ireland and indeed further afield, the Prix was the setting for one of the sport's most famous races – a mesmerising duel between Robert on the rasping black Norton and Joey on the Honda in 1990. Our wee town of Ballymoney was gripped by a palpable sense of excitement in the week leading up to that year's Ulster Grand Prix and the clash of the two brothers at Dundrod. Scottish star Steve Hislop had been the race favourite but was forced out on the opening lap, leaving Robert and Joey to go head-to-head at the front. There was little between the pair as they swapped places at the front, treating the thousands of partisan fans to a breathtaking display of close-quarters racing. Picking a winner was practically impossible but as they appeared out of the Quarry Bends virtually joined at the hip, Robert veered off to his right and into the pits to take on fuel, leaving Joey clear in the lead. The wily Joseph had timed his race to perfection and completed the entire distance on the less thirsty Honda RC30 without making any pit stops. It was an important win for Joey, marking his first major victory on a big bike since a crash at Brands Hatch in 1989 when he was struck by Stéphane Mertens.

However, perhaps the most memorable Ulster Grand Prix of all time for me involved a race in the 125cc class, in 1993,

A picture that I treasure: me on my dad Jim's knee; my brother Lawrence on my mum's, outside the cottage on the Enagh Road in Ballymoney where I grew up.

Another special picture – it must have been taken on a Sunday as Mum, Lawrence and I are all dressed up for church.

Lawrence and me ready for a football game – with clean shorts, so this was definitely taken before the start of play.

Four generations: my mum; my daughter Janice; my granny Sarah; and me.

At my son Robbie's eighteenth birthday: back row (L–R) Janice, son William and daughter Lynsey; front row (L–R) me, son Robbie, and my wife Gillian.

The beginning of a small but very successful team: sponsor Patsy (PJ) O'Kane, Robert and me at a launch event.

Joey, Robert and me on the grid on the North West 200, Robert's most successful circuit.

After the Macau Grand Prix, we always stopped off in Hong Kong for a week, a city steeped in culture – and a long way from the Toon. We never missed a visit to the famed Kowloon markets – the silk ties were always a favourite present to bring home. My good friend Jackie Fullerton has been the recipient of many over the years.

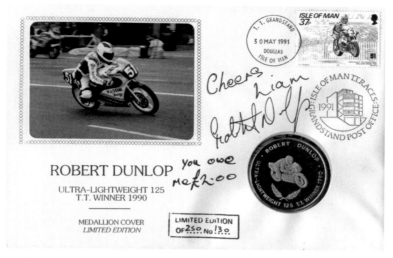

ROBERT DUNLOP

ULTRA-LIGHTWEIGHT 125
T.T. WINNER 1990

MEDALLION COVER
LIMITED EDITION

LIMITED EDITION
OF 250. No 130.

The £2 coin that was minted for Robert at the TT. He bought it for me but – typical Rob – he wanted the money back!

Some words of encouragement from me to a pensive Robert just before the start of the Cookstown 100.

Lawrence and Louise, my son and daughter from my first marriage.

My uncle Jackie and me in the scrutineering bay at the Isle of Man TT.

In the Rotherham Hotel in Douglas. An injured Robert with his wife Louise having a laugh during a rare relaxation period.

Both boys on the podium – a familiar enough spot for them.

Time to get into the zone for both of us as we prepare for the North West 200.

Robert and his twin sister Margaret at their joint 40th birthday party. Robert was one of seven children who, along with their parents, loved a family get-together.

Robert and me at the Isle of Man TT. In the background, you can see a rather youthful Jamie Whitham.

when three of the best pilots on the wee machines I have ever had the pleasure of watching engaged in by far the greatest road race that I have ever seen. Robert, Joey and an English rider called Mick Lofthouse from Lancashire served up an incredible three-way dice for the lead, taking turns at the front at practically ever corner. Some months beforehand, Joey had remarked that Lofthouse was a superb talent and one to keep an eye on, which was rare praise indeed because Joey seldom commented on another rider's potential. Lofthouse was tragically killed at the age of twenty-eight during a crash in practice at the Isle of Man TT in 1996 when he came off at Milntown on his 250cc Yamaha, apparently caught out by the glare of the sun in the days when practice was still held early in the mornings on the island. A former British 125cc champion, his untimely passing was a real loss to the sport, but what a talent he was. I was perched on a kerb at the start and finish area that day alongside highly respected motorcycle journalist, the late Jimmy Walker, and on the final lap, you could have heard a pin drop as the fans in the packed grandstands held their breath. Everyone was straining their necks to see whose helmet would appear first from the hedgerows on the exit of the final right-hander on to the finish straight to flash pass the chequered flag. The race was held at the time when the controversial chicane, first introduced in 1992, was in place before the start and finish straight, providing the last chance to make a final pass at the end of the lap. I recall Jimmy Walker leaning over and asking me who I thought would win. 'Don't ask me silly questions, Jimmy. Robert, of course,' I replied confidently, but it was a rather tongue in cheek prediction because it was anyone's guess. The commentators around the historic course, which held Grand Prix World Championship status from 1949 to 1971, were beside themselves with excitement at the action unfolding before their eyes and in a blink three riders seemed appeared in unison. To everyone's surprise, Mick Lofthouse – who'd made a mistake on the final lap – had been replaced by Phelim Owens on the dash to the line, and Robert got the verdict by no more than half a wheel. You could have thrown a blanket over the trio as they made their dash for the line that day and it was a privilege to have witnessed world-class riders putting on such a show. Rob later remarked that it was the best 125cc race he had ever competed in.

Another close race between Robert and Joey took place as we travelled to Dundrod on race morning for the Ulster Grand Prix one year. Rather than pitting their wits against each other on two wheels, the boys decided to challenge each other in their respective race vans. We had called at Joey's that Saturday morning on an errand and as we were leaving, Joey and his crew were also just pulling out from his house in his van. It didn't take long before both wagons were being pushed to their limits as Joey, at the wheel of his van, and Robert attempted to outdo one another on the trip to Dundrod. With no clear advantage, a bout of slipstreaming was required on the Ballymena bypass and it certainly wasn't a ride for the fainthearted. I was scared at times but not enough that the hilarity of the situation didn't leave me in stitches as both vans drew alongside each other with the two boys gesturing at each other, bearing grins as wide as Lough Neagh. It is a memory to cherish. Incidentally the 'race' was decided in Joey's favour, who managed to out-brake Rob into the tight hairpin on the actual Dundrod course before we made the final run towards the paddock area. It was another snapshot of their competitive nature – whatever activity they engaged in, one always wanted to beat the other.

It was on our way home from the Ulster Grand Prix one year that Robert and I had one of our most unpleasant experiences in racing. We had only just left the main paddock and were making our way towards the town of Antrim some ten miles away with a good friend, Robert Taggart. Rob was at the wheel of the PJ O'Kane Ulsterbus and I had just poured myself a cup of tea at the back when I became aware of the bus braking hard and swerving slightly. Then I heard Robert shouting something to the effect of, 'That shit just cut me off there.' Rob had flashed the lights at the offending motorist, who had now pulled in to the side of the road and was waving us down. We pulled over and the guy arrived at the entrance door to the bus, which was air-operated by means of a small button on the floor beside the driver's left foot. The guy was banging on the door and Robert activated the button to let him in. No sooner had he done so than the guy stormed on to the bus and launched into a verbal tirade at Rob, who explained he had merely flashed his lights because he had been forced to hit the brakes and take evasive action. The guy was having none of it and it was quite clear at this point that he was most definitely not a Robert Dunlop fan. It turned out that he was also on his way home from the races but that famous camaraderie so prevalent within the road racing fraternity was non-existent as he continued to berate Rob and became increasingly rude.

I supped on my cuppa as I listened to what was being said and decided it was time to speak up, so I asked him what his problem was and told him to clear off. He responded by saying something like 'make me', so I pushed my cup of tea to the side and marched towards the front of the bus. It wasn't in my DNA to back down and he was still mouthing off at Rob as I approached them. Then I heard him say, 'I hope the next time I see you is in a box.' This was a disgraceful thing to say to anyone, never mind a road racer who faced the threat of death on a regular basis. It was the final straw for me. I offered him an ultimatum: 'Get off the bus or I will rearrange your features – the choice is yours.' He took a swing at me but he missed and I caught him with a big right hook. He fell backwards out the door and stumbled through a large thorn hedge at the side of the road; all we could see of him were the soles of his Dr Marten boots protruding from the hedge. Unbeknownst to me, his female friend was outside being restrained by big Robert Taggart, as she made a significant effort to attack me with her handbag. In the middle of this furore, Joey's manager, Davy Wood, pulled in behind our bus thinking we had broken down. Rob explained what had happened and pointed to the guy lying in the hedge, and Davy, typically, was distraught. He hated any type of confrontation.

Another couple had stopped at the scene and, along with Davy, they trailed rent-a-mouth out of the hedge. He was already sporting a promising big shiner. He stormed towards his car shouting, 'I'll have you for this', and was simulating the shooting of a gun.

With the drama over, we got back on the bus and drove off, although big Taggart suggested we should make a stop at Antrim police station and report the incident. It turned out his suggestion was an inspired one because as we pulled into the car park beside the police station, who did we spot but the guy we'd just had the trouble with. Once again he simulated holding a gun at his head and shouted over, 'That's for you.' We made our way inside and were asked to explain the circumstances of what had happened. Then we were asked to take a seat on some chairs in the corridor outside one of the interview rooms. We could hear the commotion inside as the man and his female companion, who turned out to be his wife, were yelling and roaring about what happened. It was hard not to see the funny side of it and although we were able to conduct ourselves in a serious manner as we waited our turn, it was impossible not to erupt into laughter when the corridor outside echoed with the woman's exasperated pleas to her husband: 'Show him the thorns in your arse! Show him the thorns in your arse!' His backside obviously resembled a pincushion and even the officer standing outside was unable to resist a smile. Eventually, we were brought in for questioning but as we expected, the officer in charge decided no further action needed to be taken. We left the police station and finally set off on our way home again. We had many a laugh about it afterwards but the more I thought about it, the more I felt rent-a-mouth got off lightly after what he had said to Robert.

Dundrod produced plenty of happier times too. One of the best came from the late Aubrey McAuley, a fair road racer himself. Aubrey had been cresting the top of the Deer's Leap in practice and was pushing on as hard as he possibly could when two bikes flashed past him on either side in mid-air. One was Joey and the other was Robert, both racing flat-out at one of the most notorious sections of the Dundrod course. Aubrey watched dumbstruck as Robert reached over with one hand and patted Joey on the bum after they had landed. There was Aubrey holding on for grim death with both hands, yet Rob had the audacity to pat Joey's backside as they raced side-by-side. 'You scared the shit out of me up there at the Deer's Leap, Robert,' Aubrey said, when he came to our van after the session. Quick as a flash, Robert answered, 'Joey's pension book was slipping out of his back pocket.'

Both boys absolutely loved racing at Dundrod and Robert always felt he had the upper hand over Joey on the first part of the circuit, although he admitted that Joey held all the aces around the back section. They each enjoyed plenty of success at the race – Joey still holds the record for the most victories ever with twenty-four wins while Robert stood on the top step of the podium nine times in all.

A feature of the Ulster Grand Prix for us was our annual stop at the Wayside Inn pub on the way home. We always received VIP treatment from the landlady of the establishment, Bernie Byrne, who ushered us into a small front room where she'd laid on freshly made sandwiches. Bernie was always very good to us and we had so much craic in there after the races, with many of the fans who had been at Dundrod calling in on their way home in the knowledge that it was a favourite watering hole for Joey and Robert. It offered the boys a chance to unwind and relax with a few pints after a hard day's racing and it was fascinating to hear their take on events. It was certainly an eye-opener to gain the inside track on what was happening out on the course.

Within our group, our friend Robert Taggart was teetotal, which meant I had the chance to have one or two pints with the boys if I felt like it. One night after Joey had left he rang to inform us that the police were parked in a lay-by not far along the road. It seemed likely that someone had tipped them off that we were in the bar, guessing that some of us would be a good bet for a drink-driving charge. Joey and Robert had many fans, but sadly there were also those who resented their success and popularity. Sure enough, we encountered the cops on our drive home and big Taggart, who was of course at the wheel, was breathalysed at the side of the road. We weren't in the slightest bit concerned given that Robert wasn't a drinker, but the disappointment of the police was evident. Instead they discovered a defective tail light and booked us for that.

Eight
The North West 200

The North West 200 was Robert's favourite race and it suited his technique perfectly. Even to this day, hand on heart, he is still the best rider I have ever seen in action around the Triangle circuit. Robert loved the buzz and the razzmatazz around the event, which pitted many of the big names in England against our own home-grown crop of road racing specialists. He had an extra spring in his step during the week of the race, whereas I think the event had the opposite effect on Joey, who much preferred to do things in a lower key. In that respect, the two boys were polar opposites. In the earlier days Joey was the star attraction wherever he went and rightly so, because he was easily the number one road racer in the world. Joey's status meant that, by and large, Robert was able to slip into the paddocks unnoticed, although there were always a few fans who would call round to the back of the van for an autograph or a chat. It was a different scenario wherever Joey pulled up, and his van and tent were always surrounded by the largest crowds of onlookers.

In the mid-eighties it was Billy Nutt who was in charge of the North West 200, with Mervyn Whyte – who is the main man at the helm of the event today – acting as Nutt's deputy. It was Mervyn's job to come knocking on the door of our race van early in the season to attempt to sign Robert up for the North West, the first of the big international road races of the season, held in May. Robert usually played hard to get but he had two major weak spots when it came to his efforts to secure some appearance money. The first was that he wasn't a major star at the time: Joey was the big name, along with some of the riders who were enticed to make the trip over from England. The other factor was that it was widely known how much he enjoyed competing at the North West; that he would turn up and race for nothing if it came to the crunch. So it is safe to say that he had limited bargaining power.

Mervyn usually started making approaches to riders at the Cookstown 100 meeting, which for years has been the first race on the Irish road racing calendar. On other occasions he would turn up at some of the early British championship rounds in England but wherever Mervyn would present himself, Rob always said to me, 'You deal with him, LB, and don't be backwards about asking for money or else I won't be there.' Robert was only kidding himself: he'd have walked to Portrush to race at the North West if he had to because it was his race. For as long as I can remember, rumours circulated in the paddock at the North West about how much the overseas riders were being paid to compete at the event and, as you can imagine, this didn't sit well with the local stars. Robert always felt that because he and Joey only lived a few miles away from the circuit and were regulars at almost every race, their participation was taken for granted. They were not offered the financial sweeteners thrown the way of the English and European racers.

He had a point, but my response to him was always the same: start winning. If Robert could establish himself as a regular race winner then the ball would be in his court when it came to negotiating a deal the following season. It was inevitable that

Rob would prove successful at the North West because it seemed as though he was made for the place and, sure enough, his big breakthrough came in 1986 when he won the 350cc race on a Formula 2 Yamaha sponsored by Ken Dundee. A number of people were instrumental in helping Robert in those early days and Ken was one of them along with Geoffrey Alexander and the Taggarts. Without them, it would have been virtually impossible to start a race never mind finish one and although, at that time, the 350cc class did not carry the same prestige as some of the other races, Robert had still registered his maiden victory at one of the big three majors. It was a pivotal moment in his career and the first of his fifteen wins at the North West, which made him the most successful rider ever in the history of the event. His record was only equalled in 2015 by fellow Northern Ireland man Alastair Seeley – bearing in mind that Robert was restricted to the smaller 125cc machines after his career-changing accident in 1994, it is testament to his brilliance that his record stood for so long.

His 1986 victory was a special day for him, but it was four years later in 1990 when Robert really made people sit up and take notice. He recorded a magnificent hat-trick of wins, which included a brace of victories in the prestigious Superbike class on the iconic all-black JPS Norton machine. The image of Robert manhandling the 588cc Rotary Norton around the 8.9-mile course has become the stuff of legend and, without question, remains one of the standout wins in the long history of the event. His treble was competed with a win in the 125cc class. Robert had announced his arrival on the big stage in some style, rewarding those who had stood by him and kept faith in his talent. Although Robert would become the undisputed king of the North West, it wasn't all plain sailing at his home race. Many will recall the incident in 1989 when he was hit from behind by another rider at Metropole Corner in Portrush and taken to Coleraine Hospital. It was common knowledge that Robert's injuries weren't serious or life-threatening in any way – he had been fortunate to escape with severe bruising and some loss of skin – but Joey still came to the hospital in person to make sure that Rob was okay before he made his way on home.

Although I was certain that Robert had the talent to get to the very top in his chosen profession, it wasn't until 1990 that others began to share my optimism. He was becoming more confident by the day and I had now been at his side long enough to ensure that his focus on the job in hand was absolute. Robert followed up his 1990 hat-trick with another three wins at the North West the following year, this time winning his first race in the ultra-competitive 250cc class at a time when it was packed with stars: Joey, Brian Reid, Eddie Laycock, Ian Newton, Jim Moodie, Steve Hislop and Phillip McCallen. In fact, any one of up to twenty riders were capable of winning, such was the depth of talent in the field, but Robert came out on top to reach another milestone in his career. His win on the 250 gave him a full collection of trophies across the 125cc, 250cc, 350cc and Superbike classes at the North West; it was an incredible achievement for a sportsman who had done it the hard way. His second successive treble also consisted of another Superbike victory on the JPS Norton and victory in the 125cc race. After years of scrimping and saving, sacrifices and hand-me-downs, Robert was now a world-class road racer in his own right and, at last, he knew it.

Rob's stock may have been in the ascendancy, and although he now shared a top-level reputation with Joey, he still looked up to his older brother, who remained his idol. Even though he was now beating Joey in major road races, Joey was still the king to him – the best ever – and Rob was his biggest fan. Joey now fully realised that his wee brother was a major threat at every race they entered together, but that didn't stop him offering his advice and support. He confided in me that Robert was the best 125cc rider there had ever been on both the short circuits and the roads and he genuinely meant it.

Given Robert's notable success, more doors were beginning to open, new sponsors were appearing on the scene and the media interest surrounding him intensified. However, with greater success comes a heightened degree of expectation, and although I always set my sights high in terms of professionalism, we knew we had to up our game even further as Rob began to scale the road racing summit. The jeans and oil-stained T-shirts were replaced by black team trousers and shirts covered with the logos of sponsors; there were times when I felt like a professional darts player rather than a team manager and mechanic. Looking back now, it was then that a lot of the fun went out of the job and the laughter we so often shared was replaced by a more serious atmosphere, which was dominated by constant pressure to deliver top results. Securing a place on the front row of the grid was important for the sponsors, because of the media coverage, and it was not unknown for some to more or less demand that they wanted Robert at the front. These new obligations brought a whole different level of pressure to the job for Robert, who now felt he had to deliver not only in the races, but also in practice. It was a heavy burden, but it was a price we were both willing to pay as he continued on his path to stardom. I guess you could say it comes with the territory but it was something that we found ourselves having to adapt to after ploughing our own furrow for so long. More and more demands were being made on Robert's time and it wasn't uncommon for him to head off to the south of Ireland to make an appearance at another rider's fundraising event or to attend a charity event, despite his hectic schedule. Rob always tried to oblige and he gave up his time for free, certainly when charity was involved – I have always felt that Robert didn't get the recognition he deserved for this aspect of his career. In fact, on many occasions it actually cost him money to attend these events – something he could ill-afford. Robert still had a mortgage to pay and a wife and a young family to support; although he was on an upward trajectory, he wasn't yet earning big money and was only just about breaking even.

If you gave him a decent bike and conditions were dry, then Robert was virtually unbeatable around the Triangle circuit. The secret to a fast lap is to ride the slow corners slow and the fast corners fast. So many riders do the opposite, but Robert knew that there was little to be gained in the slow corners and instead focused on those parts of the course that really mattered. He had the skill and the bravery to take Mather's Cross, this frighteningly fast right-hander, flat out on the little 125cc and 250cc machines, chest flat on the tank, head buried beneath the bubble with the throttle pinned wide open. Trust me, it takes a fair set of balls and exceptional ability to accomplish such a feat. Anyone familiar with this particular part of the North West 200 course knows that the corner is situated at the end of a long straight, coming after a top gear blast from the 'Magic' roundabout at Ballysally in Coleraine all the way to Mather's. There was no easing off from Robert, who had this critical corner down to perfection, enabling him to carry his momentum all the way down to Metropole Corner in Portrush – a two-mile stretch where it's flat-out in sixth gear all the way. Today, a chicane has been added at Mather's for safety purposes and a man-made chicane has also since been created halfway between Mather's and Metropole Corner, again with the aim of slowing riders down. These safety measures are generally met with disdain by the majority of road racers, who feel they belong on short circuits and detract from the challenges involved in racing between the hedges. In 2015, the sport's biggest star – Lincolnshire rider Guy Martin – launched into a rant live on air criticising the number of chicanes around the course (there are four in total), labelling the track 'boring' and casting doubt over whether or not he would ever race there again. The presence of so many chicanes now most definitely suits the short circuit specialists and it has come as no surprise to me that leading British championship protagonist Alastair Seeley is such a special talent at the North West. He loves the circuit, it suits him and, boy, is he good around there. Alastair equalled Robert's record in May 2015 – they are now level on fifteen victories apiece and Alastair is set to become the most successful rider ever in the history of the event. I have to admit that if Robert's record was to be broken, I always wanted a Dunlop to do it, either William or Michael. I know that it sounds biased, but I saw at first hand how much toil and sweat it took for Robert to set that milestone and how many broken bones and setbacks he had to overcome in the process.

We always did our homework when it came to planning our tactics at the North West and we would visit the circuit virtually every night during race week, often in the wee small hours. In the darkness, the dipped headlights of the van helped to highlight every ripple and bump on the road surface, which helped Robert identify the smoothest racing line – information he certainly used to his full advantage. We also discussed the various braking points and Rob made a mental note of each marker: it could be a certain tree, straw bale or a distinctive piece of roadside 'furniture' – anything that would catch his eye that he could use as an indicator. His braking markers changed dependant on the machine he was riding due to the higher or lesser speeds involved in riding a 125 or a fully-fledged Superbike. This was essential preparation and Robert took this side of the job very seriously. As a 125cc British champion, Robert's short circuit experience proved invaluable at the North West, and he could scratch with the best of them on the real knee-down parts of the course. Believe me, if Rob was ahead at Metropole Corner on the final lap, no one was going to get one over on him on the run along the sweeping Coast Road section towards the start and finish line. I'd have put my house on him winning in this situation, even if it did belong to the building society at the time.

He was in an absolute class of his own along that technical final third of the North West 200 tarmac and I've yet to see anyone better – I don't think I ever will.

As you'd expect, the more races Robert won, the more prestigious his position within the main race paddock became. We were now permitted to park up near the front of the paddock, amongst the so-called big boys with their fancy transporters, right in the vicinity of the works teams and riders. In the early '90s the North West 200 organisers had taken the decision to tarmac a fairly large area of the field, which was set aside for the top names and teams. The lesser known competitors still had to make do with grass beneath their awnings and the occasional reminder that they were temporarily occupying the rightful home of a herd of cows, courtesy of those brown flat caps that had caught me out many times in the past. In fairness to the Coleraine club, they continued to improve the facilities year in, year out, and consulted the views of experienced riders if they were planning to introduce any changes to the course layout – with the safety of competitors clearly at the forefront of their minds, and I applaud them for that.

The North West is highly competitive, yet there is also a relaxed, social element to the race, which is something enjoyed by the local competitors and probably even more by those riders who take a break from the British championship scene to assume their position on the grid in Portrush. It's a week-long meeting incorporating practice and racing on three days in total, with a varied programme of entertainment laid on, creating a feel-good factor that filters through to the riders and teams as well as the thousands of fans from near and far who flock to the north coast for the week. Our preferred watering hole when Robert was racing was the York Hotel, a famous vantage point located at the slowest hairpin on the course, less than two miles from the paddock. Several other riders also frequented the same establishment for a quiet pint, although the old Sea Splash

Hotel in Portstewart was the most popular haunt, with a disco taking place most nights. The York, though, was perfect for us and we could mull over the key talking points of race week in relative peace over a beer, and it allowed Robert the chance to unwind.

Following Robert's glorious North West 200 treble in 1990 he wanted a small, private celebration so we decided to head out for dinner that night with his wife Louise and my own better half Gillian. It had become something of a tradition following race day at the North West for us to call into a local bar in town called the Portstewart Arms to enjoy a cool pint as the heavy traffic cleared away from the course. It was a great bar with good people in charge and we were always made to feel very welcome in there. So we decided to call in before we went home to collect Louise and Gillian. On this particular Saturday, there were many people in the bar who wanted to shake Robert's hand because of his brilliant performance only hours earlier. As per usual, Rob was patient and understanding and after a while we finally managed to find a seat. We had only settled down and were beginning to enjoy our pints when a woman approached us and poured a full pint of beer over Robert's head. I stared in disbelief as she roared, 'You'll never be another Joey.' The woman was blind drunk and completely soaked Rob from head to toe, but before I had a chance to tell her what I thought of her, the staff acted quickly and evicted her from the premises. To his immense credit, Robert never reacted and just continued to stare straight ahead and sip his pint; there was nothing to be gained from trying to engage with this drunken troublemaker. It transpired she had previously been thrown out of the bar for being drunk and disorderly but had somehow managed to sneak back in.

Regardless, we drank up, accepted the apologies of the staff and set sail for home for a change of clothes and to pick up our wives before heading on for a meal at the Bohill Hotel on the outskirts of Coleraine. The proprietor, whom we both knew well, seated the four of us in a nice secluded area of the dining room and we enjoyed a lovely meal together and a few drinks to celebrate what had been a day to remember for Robert. The man of the moment was in high spirits and announced that he was going to treat us, so off he went to square the bill at reception. We went outside and ordered a taxi home after a fantastic evening and all was well until my wife Gillian received a phone call on the Monday morning. The voice on the other end of the phone enquired if our meal had been satisfactory. Gillian replied that it had been wonderful, as usual, before asking why the hotel was ringing. Back came the response, 'Well, it's just that you left without paying the bill.' Gillian apologised before promising she would look into it. It transpired that Robert, on his way to pick up the tab to treat us all, had bumped into some fans who wanted autographs and a chat. He duly obliged but completely forgot to head on to reception and pay the bill. Robert was almost as embarrassed as Gillian was when she phoned him with the news, but needless to say he quickly made his way back to the hotel to settle up. We could all see the funny side of it afterwards and Rob took no end of stick for his oversight over the years.

Robert's achievements on the Norton stand out as among my most cherished memories of the North West 200. The all-black JPS-sponsored machine holds a special place in the heart of all road racing fans and a famous picture from the time taken by Clifford McLean perfectly encapsulates the magic of the era, with Robert, and Joey on the Honda, side-by-side at the 'Magic' Roundabout in Coleraine. Rob always said it was his favourite machine and he absolutely loved riding it. He was desperate to seize his chance and delivered in style for Norton, claiming a dominant double in 1990 and adding another prized Superbike win the following year. In fact, if it hadn't been for a mechanical problem in 1991, Rob would have wrapped up another double but fate intervened and he retired just after Mather's Cross.

His success for the iconic British manufacturer didn't come without its fair share of drama behind the scenes, though. The Rotary-engined Norton was unquestionably a complete rocket in a straight line and Rob was unofficially clocked at more than 200mph on the flat-out section from Station Corner to University in Coleraine. While the outright speed of the thing was never in doubt, and it was certainly a superb motorcycle, it was no secret that it wasn't the sweetest handling machine on the grid; to put it another way, at times it was like a bucking bronco. I used to joke with Rob that I could even see it weaving from side to side as they wheeled it down the plank from the back of the transporter. The problem was exaggerated by the fact that Robert was so small and light. In 1990 one section of the course in particular was proving problematic. The long straight from the 'Magic' Roundabout all the way down to Mather's Cross was proving troublesome for Robert – the sheer torque and power of the 588cc engine meant he was fighting it all the way to stop the front wheel pawing the air as he accelerated through the gears. The front-end was pointing skywards each time he clicked another gear, with the end result that when Rob eventually hit sixth, the front wheel was returning to the surface of the tarmac on an especially bumpy stretch of the road at a row of small cottages not far from his entry point into the fearsome right-hander at Mather's. Each time the bike would become extremely unsettled, resulting in a few major tank-slappers throughout practice. We drove out to this part of the course to inspect the rippled section of road responsible for causing Rob a few heart-stopping moments. As usual, we carried out our inspection at night, using dipped headlights to illuminate the imperfections on the road. Robert was losing quite a lot of time here because he was forced to shut off the throttle to bring the Norton back under control when the tank-slappers kicked in, therefore costing him maximum drive through Mather's and on to the long straight towards Metropole Corner a few miles down the road. We tried everything to find a solution and Rob experimented with several different lines, but to no avail. Norton's suspension expert back then was former Honda employee Ron Williams and we drew on his expertise to see if there was a compromise with the setting that would make a difference, but again we ultimately drew a blank. Such was the level of opposition, the time Rob was losing here could prove to be the difference between winning and losing. The grid was packed with major names, including Carl Fogarty, Eddie Laycock, Phillip McCallen, Rob's Norton team-mate Trevor Nation and of course Joey.

Race day morning loomed and we still hadn't managed to find an answer. Rob was concerned about the race ahead and so was I – this beast of a machine could be hitting speeds of 170mph at the point where it began to shake its head violently. For once, we didn't have a Plan B and my nerves were shredded as the massive crowds of expectant fans began to arrive around the course and the tension inched up hour by hour. The stage was set, the inevitable moment arrived, and I watched as Robert lowered his visor and set off on his warm-up lap before the start of the opening Superbike race. I knew inside how much he wanted to provide Norton and, more importantly, Norton boss Barry with a victory that day because he had given him a superb opportunity. It seemed like an eternity before the riders returned to begin lining up on the grid. As I approached him to give his visor one final wipe and clean off any dead flies, he told me, 'I've got it sorted, LB. There's no need to worry.' I couldn't believe my ears because we had been banging our heads against a brick wall in our efforts to find a solution to tame the bike.

The signal came to clear the grid and after I gave my usual message to Rob, I moved off to the side of the grid to watch the start of the race. The starter's flag dropped and with a thunderous roar the first group disappeared into the distance as they made their way down to York Corner for the first time. Robert swapped places with Carl Fogarty on the opening laps before pulling away to win in style, and the rest is history. He completed a double with another commanding win in race two and to put it simply, no one could live with him and the Norton that day – they were an unbeatable combination. Barry and everyone in the Norton team were ecstatic and it was just rewards for the faith they had put in him. They gave him the tools and Rob got the job done in emphatic fashion. They were good lads at Norton.

I could hardly hide my impatience as I waited for my chance to ask Robert how the hell he had managed to solve the tank-slapper puzzle on the approach to Mather's. He told me that on the warm-up lap he simply decided to bite the bullet, opting to dig his knees tightly and firmly into the slight recesses on each side of the fuel tank, pull his elbows in as close against his ribcage as possible and keep the throttle pinned flat open. It was a courageous decision but thankfully it paid off and although Rob admitted he was more than a little apprehensive when he tried it the first time, once the strategy worked, he knew he could repeat it again and again. The solution was simply to grin and bear it and full credit to Rob for having the balls to pull it off.

For now, the world was a beautiful place and Rob and the Norton team seemed a match made in heaven. By and large all the Norton lads were good to Robert, but Barry more so than anyone else. He was a proper motorcycle team manager and his attention to detail was second to none. It seemed like only yesterday that Robert was confirmed in the works JPS Norton team and he was like a kid at Christmas. He was overjoyed that he had arrived at the big time with a works team prepared to take a chance on him and he couldn't wait to show me the pristine new team attire. He was stood there in my kitchen, grinning from ear to ear, in the official Norton team shirt and I was absolutely delighted for him because he had finally got what he deserved. Everything about the deal seemed right and I was particularly pleased that Barry was the team boss because I knew that, deep down, he was a Dunlop man and would have Rob's best interests at heart. As it turned out, though, Robert's Norton career proved short-lived as the factory, based in Lichfield in Staffordshire, was in financial trouble. It was becoming increasingly difficult for Norton to sustain a race team and Robert had to search for a new ride after two great years with the British concern.

He was eventually to link up with Medd Racing to ride a Honda RC45. The Medd lads were two fantastic guys and, just as had been the case at Norton, we immediately gelled with the team and Rob soon proved his ability to adapt to new machinery. He was one of the most versatile riders of his generation, capable of winning on the smallest 125cc machines before jumping on a full-blown 750cc Superbike and repeating the feat all in the same day. The quality of the opposition in the early nineties was staggering: in both the two-stroke classes and the prestigious Superbike races, the grids were crammed full of world-class talent. Robert was in an elite bracket of riders who were able to rise to the occasion on the biggest stages of all and beat the best; more often than not, he took them all on and chinned them – I've always loved using that word to describe his very greatest performances. So many of our leading riders won week in, week out at the grassroots Irish National road races throughout Ireland, and I commend them for that, but what set the likes of Robert and Joey apart was that they had that something extra special that enabled them to win at the three majors. It was all well and good taking the top prize at meetings such as the Cookstown 100 or Tandragee, but when many of the world's best motorcycle riders arrived in Portrush each May, only a special few had what it took in their armoury to step up and face down the challenge of these big overseas stars. Robert certainly fell into that exclusive category. The Dunlops were different and they have the statistics on their records to prove it; this is what elevated them to the status of world-class competitors.

Robert went on to further polish his burgeoning reputation as the undisputed king of the North West 200 with a treble in the 125cc and 250cc races in 1993 before clinching a Superbike double on the Medd Honda RC45 in 1994 – giving Honda's new 750cc machine its maiden international victories in the process as he defeated Iain Duffus and Phillip McCallen respectively in the two big races of the day. He completed yet another hat-trick that day with an almost customary success in the 125cc race, leading home Phelim Owens and Kevin Mawdsley. At this point in his career, I felt Robert was probably in the best form of his life. Away from the paddock, he had a happy home life with a young family he adored and he was gaining the recognition he had worked so hard for. In my opinion, Robert – already a very special rider – was now on the verge of greatness and I would not have ruled out a move to the World Superbike Championship or indeed to Grand Prix racing in the 125cc class because he was that good. Sadly, such is the nature of the sport, it is impossible to predict the future. Little did we know what lay around the corner.

Nine
The Mighty Micro

Without question, the Isle of Man TT circuit is the most dangerous of them all. We used to travel to it across the Irish Sea by boat each year, in a fishing boat in the early days and then via the Isle of Man ferry. Although it was quite a short trip in terms of distance, the journey used to take around five-and-a-half hours because of the route – but we rarely noticed the passage of time because of the variety of characters on board. Michael Swann, a fantastic short circuit rider in his day, was a magnificent harmonica player and when he was around, it was never long before a sing-song was in full flow. Aubrey McAuley also loved a good party and was always up for a laugh; Aubrey was a great lad and if you ever needed help nothing was too much trouble. When Aubrey lost his life after a crash during practice for the Killalane road races in 1997, Rob and I packed up and headed for home immediately. All deaths in road racing are regrettable, but Aubrey's fatal accident was particularly hard to come to terms with because we had been very friendly not only with Aubs, but also with his family. It was hard to deal with and Robert took Aubrey's death really hard; he barely spoke a word for days afterwards.

Once we'd arrived in the Isle of Man, we based ourselves at a hotel called The Rotherham and were very lucky to receive free accommodation thanks to the generosity of the proprietors, Reg and June McDowell. They treated us like family from day one and, in the early days, Joey and his team stayed there too, plus the boys' father Willie and Jackie Graham. I'd have shared a room with Jackie while Robert and his dad had a room together. We were so well looked after and Reg and June's daughter Karen was an absolute gem. She used to make sure that Robert's leathers and helmet were immaculate and joined us for the 5 a.m. practice mornings, and would have fixed us breakfast afterwards back at the hotel before she went to work.

Rob's family rarely made the trip to the TT, although occasionally his wife Louise travelled to the island for a few days with my wife Gillian. Robert and Joey's mum May also made the odd visit but she usually stayed at home in Ballymoney to avoid complicating the boys' preparations. Robert's father Willie always came with us and did his best to split his time equally between Rob and Joey. He was a motor mechanic by trade and, just like his boys, he was extremely gifted when it came to mechanical know-how and wasn't afraid to offer his opinion. Sadly, there were those outside the Dunlop family who tried to portray Willie as having a favourite son but these people were ill-informed to say the least. Willie was equally devoted to both boys and their careers, which is why it makes me cross when people suggest otherwise. The same applies to the boys' only surviving brother, Jim, who I never witnessed showing favouritism to one or the other. Both Willie and Jim understood how vitally important it was that only the proper people were around the boys during race time. The wrong type were politely ignored in the hope that they would move on because this is not a sport that needs hangers-on and both Joey and Rob had their fair share of them over the years.

In the eighties, Joey worked from a garage at the bottom of Bray Hill owned by the McCanney family, who were originally from Northern Ireland, which he shared with Robert. However, once Rob began to get more bikes of his own, Joey – gentleman that he was – moved to larger garage premises down near the harbour in Douglas. Both teams would always meet up at night once our preparations for the next day were complete. We went to a hotel on the seafront and generally everyone only had a pint the night before a race or practice session. It was an absolute education being able to sit there and listen to Joey and Rob talk so intimately about every corner on the legendary TT Mountain Course, and discuss how practice had gone earlier in the day. Joey taught Robert a lot and Rob certainly appreciated the advice because Joey was the greatest rider I have ever seen around the TT circuit. I've seen many brilliant riders on the course – especially McGuinness, Anstey, Hutchinson and Rutter – but Joey was the undisputed king of the island not only in my eyes, but he was in Robert's too.

It wasn't only Joey's extraordinary ability that enabled him to beat the rest at the TT, it was also his sheer concentration. I have never seen a rider more focused during a pit stop at the TT than Joey. Our pit box was usually next to Joey's and it gave us a close-up view of how the great man acted when he came in for fuel and fresh tyres. His eyes were so focused with intent and he just stared down the pit lane until it was time to fire the bike up again and set off on another lap; he never spoke a word unless someone made a cock-up. Rob found it hard to maintain complete focus throughout the duration of a TT race – a gruelling six laps of the 37.73-mile course in the Formula One and Senior races. One lap of the legendary circuit is equivalent to a whole 125cc race at the North West 200. In particular, Rob struggled on laps five and six at the TT and, even though he'd have been approaching speeds of close to 200mph, Rob told me that his mind would sometimes wander towards the end of a race. Incredibly, he could start thinking about the most trivial things such as mowing the lawn when he returned home. We were talking about this subject one night with our good friend Eddie Layock. Eddie agreed that Joey's ability to maintain such high levels of concentration was a key strength and confided in us that he, too, had struggled with this, especially on the run over the Snaefell Mountain section, which is quite open and repetitive. In fact, Eddie revealed that he used to hum Elvis Presley's 'Are You Lonesome Tonight?' to help him stay alert. I doubt many people who watched Eddie flying past them at the TT could have imagined he'd be humming one of the King's old hits!

One night after TT practice Rob and I met up with Joey and his squad for a shandy on the promenade. We went to a hotel that had a quieter back lounge, which suited us perfectly because Joey never really enjoyed being amongst large crowds. When we arrived the front bar was packed with girls who were taking part in a hockey competition in Douglas. We went through to the back lounge, where Joey perched himself at the bar with my uncle Jackie, while Robert and I sat down on the floor with our backs against the wall. Word soon reached the front bar that the great Joey Dunlop was inside and before long a girl, with a fantastic figure I might add, walked straight up to Joe and asked him to sign the bottom of her back. Joey obliged and carried on his conversation with Jackie and the cheers went up when the girl went back out to her friends. Then, maybe around ten minutes later, she came back in, lifted up her top and asked Joey to sign her breasts. Needless to say Joey was having none of it and away she went, this time arriving back to the front lounge to an even bigger cheer. We were having a laugh and a joke about it when lo and behold the lass came back in again, but this time she had taken off her bra and hoisted up her top to reveal a quite superb pair of boobs before saying, 'Will you sign them now Joey?' Clearly more embarrassed than anything, Joey said, 'No chance – you're pushing your luck now.' We were in fits of laughter over it and I asked Rob what he would've done. He had no hesitation in saying he'd have signed them without the girl having to ask twice and then remarked, 'There you go, LB, our Joey has all the luck.' A few nights later we were in the Villa Marina in Douglas for one of the prize-giving events. I was standing talking to Jason Griffiths, a racer and great friend, when he nudged me and said, 'I think Robert wants you, LB.' I looked over and there was a large man down on his knees getting Rob to sign his bald head. 'What did I tell you?' Rob shouted. 'Our Joey has all the luck.'

Robert was something special on the 125cc two-strokes at the TT. The 125cc class, or Ultra Lightweight race as it was called, was reintroduced at the TT in 1989 after being dropped from the schedule following the 1974 meeting. The race for the wee bikes was held over four laps of the Mountain Course, requiring one pit stop. In the earlier days his father Willie was in charge of refuelling while I looked after the screen and visor, making sure they were clean and free of any dirt and flies. I also checked the chain and pushed Robert out of the pit box once he was ready to set off. Pit stops at the TT are a crucial part of the race and victory can be secured or lost in those few seconds, but Willie was always as cool as a cucumber and it was one thing less for Robert to worry about because he trusted both of us to get he job done. He confessed to me that he felt comforted as he headed down the Mountain on his 'slowing-down lap' to come into the pits knowing that we were waiting for him: he told me, 'LB you have no idea how reassuring it is to know you boys are there.' Mind you, praise was something Rob rarely offered verbally but it was always clear from his body language whether or not he was happy and if he wasn't, he would soon have made that abundantly clear: anyone guilty of incompetence got short-shrift from Rob. Mutual respect and trust between rider and mechanic is crucial in this sport.

I always believed in meticulous preparation before a race and this was taken to the extreme by Rob at the TT. He attempted to sharpen up his knowledge of the Mountain Course by driving around it in the van in the early hours of the morning when the roads were so much quieter. You could identify so many more bumps on the road under the headlights and some of those laps could've been pretty hairy. How we avoided tipping the van over I'll never know.

In 1989, there was no better rider than Robert in this class in the United Kingdom or Ireland – he was the clear number one. However one rider caught Rob's attention and, as we were checking the lap times from the earlier practice session, Rob said to me, 'Keep an eye out for that boy Ian Lougher, LB. He's going rightly.' We hadn't heard of him until then, but it wasn't long before we knew exactly who he was.

That same year Joey had suffered serious injuries in a crash at Brands Hatch following a collision with the Belgian rider Stéphane Mertens at Paddock Hill Bend. He remained determined to compete at the TT, but failed to pass the thorough medical assessment at Noble's Hospital and was ruled out of that year's event. The first Rob and I knew of it was when we were working in the garage at the bottom of Bray Hill. We had the door closed because it was a cold day and the next thing the door opened and there was Joey on crutches. With Joey unable to participate, he told Robert to go up to the grandstand immediately to see if he could get the allocation of Michelin tyres that had been set aside for Joey for the 125cc race. At that stage, we had to buy our own tyres, whereas Joey received an abundance of top class rubber from Michelin. We immediately downed tools and drove the short distance up to the grandstand, parked up and made our way to the Michelin race office to find Roger Davenport, who was the man in charge at the time. He always struck me as someone who never fitted in with the road racing scene – for a start, he was far too posh and was always decked out in full corporate attire, with a Michelin-branded shirt and more badges on him than you'd see in a whole series of *Blue Peter*. I explained to Roger that, with Joey being ruled out of the race, perhaps he could provide Rob with the allocation of Michelins that had been earmarked for Joey. The response wasn't exactly what we had wanted to hear as Roger informed us, 'I'm afraid I've already allocated those to Phillip McCallen.' We were both stumped, but I fired back, 'Would you not want the winner of the 125cc TT race to be using Michelins?' He smugly replied, 'Don't worry, I already have the winner'. I nearly took the door off the hinges on the way out and Robert was gutted to have missed out. His preference at that time was for Michelin rubber, but after the way he'd been treated he said, 'Right, LB, get the Dunlop stickers out and get them on the wee lady. We'll sicken them.'

Robert was a shrewd customer, but he was also very stubborn and he was determined to switch to Dunlop tyres for the race to get one over on Davenport and Michelin. I made it clear that if he believed he had a better chance of winning the race using a Michelin front tyre then he should go with his instinct and swallow his pride. Reliable performance from both tyres is key but especially so when it came to choosing the front tyre on a 125 at the TT. Changing a front tyre during a 125cc race at the TT would've been unheard of because time is always of the essence, so selection of the correct rubber compound was absolutely vital. The front wheel steers the bike, after all, and where a rider has a chance of controlling a rear-wheel slide, if the front lets go it spells disaster most of the time. I didn't want Robert's stubbornness to affect his judgement, but right up until the night before the race he was still toying with the idea of running a Dunlop front, even though I knew his preference was for the Michelin. I told him the time had come to let his head rule his heart and so he hatched a plan as a compromise. We plastered the bike with as many Dunlop stickers as we could lay our hands on, fitted a Dunlop front tyre to our spare wheel, walked the bike through scrutineering and parked her up in the warm-up area. Rob knew only too well that Davenport would be roaming around with his clipboard, making notes on what rubber the top contenders had chosen for the race. He'd probably assumed we'd opted for Michelins in spite of what had happened but what a shock he must've got when he walked up to our bike and realised it was shod with Dunlops, front and rear. I watched from a distance as he wandered over for a look at our bike with his pen in hand. Once he'd gone I quickly made my way to the wee lady and set about replacing the spare front wheel with our proper wheel, which was fitted with a brand new Michelin tyre.

Robert went out and won the race by fifteen seconds from Ian Lougher, with Carl Fogarty finishing third. Davenport's predicted winner, Phillip McCallen, finished the race in seventh. Dunlop tyres received all the plaudits after Robert's victory – his first ever win at the TT – which unbeknownst to anyone other than ourselves had been gained using a Michelin on the front. I saw Sir Davenport in parc fermé following the race and his face was as white as his shirt. I couldn't resist a wee dig so, as I walked past, I whispered in his ear, 'Put that in your pipe and smoke it, big fellow.' He looked at me with a face like thunder and it came as no surprise the following season when I learned that Davenport's expertise was now being put to use by Michelin in the car racing scene.

The whole episode was a stark reminder that we faced a very difficult task if Rob was to carve out his own niche and attract the sponsorship breaks he deserved. At this stage, I genuinely felt that Robert being the younger brother of Joey Dunlop was a hindrance rather than a help. The attitude of many sponsors was that they were already backing the best Dunlop, so why would they support another who was – in their opinion – not going to win as many races at he would lose at that stage of his career.

It was very frustrating and although we were very fortunate to have a great sponsor in PJ O'Kane, essentials such as tyres were putting a huge strain on our racing budget. I recall Rob winning the 125cc race at the Mid Antrim 150 one year and having to put £15 of his own cash on top of his prize-winner's cheque to cover the cost of the front tyre he had bought for the race. Racing was very much a labour of love.

One thing you can never guarantee in motorcycle road racing is any semblance of a timetable. All the best-laid plans go straight out the window as soon as mechanical problems are encountered and one such time really sticks out in my mind. It was at the TT in 1991 when one of my favourite groups, Status Quo, were due to play an open air concert at Noble's Park in Douglas. To our great surprise one day when we were working in the garage, we were informed by a guy that *Motorcycle News* wanted to do a photo shoot with Robert and Status Quo a day before the concert. Apparently the Quo were into their bikes and had specifically requested Rob for the feature. We didn't need to think twice about it so off we went with PJ O'Kane's Honda RC30 in the van. I can remember arriving at the arena and seeing this massive stage set up with all the sound systems in place for the big gig the next night. We were greeted by the main men themselves, Rick Parfitt and Francis Rossi, two down to earth guys who really fitted in with the motorcycling fraternity. They made us feel right at home and Rob even had a bang on the drums before posing for photographs with a guitar and the bike up on the stage. We spent a fabulous couple of hours with the Quo lads and they insisted that Rob and I would attend the concert the next evening as their special guests. We got two VIP backstage passes and I was absolutely over the moon. So we headed back to the garage to work on the bikes, on a complete high. However, the following day practice went badly – the 250 seized again – and we had to strip the bike down and do a complete rebuild. Bang went our hopes of attending the Status

Quo concert and to say I was gutted is an understatement. I can clearly remember sitting outside the garage at the bottom of Bray Hill that evening, washing engine parts in petrol, as Status Quo blasted out all their greatest hits in the distance. I should've been there lapping up the backstage hospitality but it wasn't to be as Rob's bikes came first. When I returned home I gave my unused VIP pass to my daughter Janice, who couldn't believe I never got the chance to put it to good use.

Any time we needed to test bikes at the TT in those early years we would make our way to Jurby airfield in the north of the island. Back then it was simply a matter of turning up and getting down to work without any interference. However, it became pretty dangerous in later years when fans would turn up to spectate while some actually joined in, taking their road bikes on to the track. It was an accident waiting to happen, especially when you consider there were 125cc machines on the track at the same time as the much more powerful Superbikes. Soon the organisers decreed that only TT competitors could gain a permit from the race office in the paddock to use the airfield and it was really the only sensible course of action under the circumstances. Believe me, when you're out there on a little 125 and a Superbike comes tearing past on the straight, it can be quite a frightening experience. I used to run in the pistons, chains and tyres for Rob at Jurby but it was never too long before he became impatient, waving me down and saying, 'That's enough now, LB. I can count the wheel spokes every time you're going past.'

I have to confess, we didn't always test at Jurby legally and in 1993 we were up against it after the 250 seized in practice. We had worked flat out to try and get the bike rebuilt for official practice the following day, but despite our best efforts we didn't complete the work until really late in the evening. It was dark at this stage and, Rob being Rob, he suggested that we take the bike to Jurby for a quick test. John Hamilton, a good friend of ours from Dervock, and someone who regularly helped us at the TT, had a hire car so we enlisted his help and headed for Jurby with Rob and me in the race van and John following in the hire car. It must have been close to midnight when we arrived and we took the 250 out of the van and got her fired up. We then parked the van at one end of the straight with its full headlights on and John did likewise at the far end with the hire car. It was far from perfect, but there was enough light to enable Rob to get his bearings, and as he blasted down the long straight, the joyous wail of the two-stroke Yamaha echoed around the surrounding countryside in the stillness of the night. As Rob increased his speeds, my attention was drawn to a flurry of rapid movements in the shadows. As my eyes adjusted, I realised that there were dozens of rabbits scurrying about all over the place and I couldn't wave down Rob quick enough – if he'd struck one of them then the consequences could've been disastrous. We were finished for the night but the drama didn't end there: as we attempted to leave the circuit we were stopped by the police. It turned out that someone living nearby had alerted the authorities to our illegal practice session and the policeman approached the driver's window of the van as we pulled out on to the main road. 'Are we doing some late night testing, sir?' he asked, to which Rob replied in the affirmative. The young bobby then enquired, 'You're Mr Dunlop, aren't you?' Rob replied that he was and the policeman then asked, 'Are you Joey?' Without a moment's hesitation, Rob answered, 'Correct again,' and the cop responded, 'Ah well, in that case, on you go, nice to meet you.' We had a great laugh about it on the way back to Douglas but we certainly never let Joey know what had happened.

Reliability is of the utmost importance at the TT and the bikes were set up to offer the best possible chance of seeing out the race distance, even if this meant sacrificing a few miles per hour in top speed. We did everything we could within the legal boundaries to gain an advantage, doubling up on exhaust springs, for example, and securing every nut and bolt with lacing wire to withstand the rigours of the thousands of bumps around the course. We even replaced the rubber engine mountings on the 125 with parts from a washing machine purchased from an electrical store on the outskirts of Douglas because we felt they were much stronger and Rob won a race at the TT using them.

There is nowhere on earth like the TT circuit. It terrified me then and it still does today. I used to ride an old 250cc Honda Superdream at home but after I came across a fatal road accident one year at the TT I sold it as soon as I arrived home. We'd been testing at Jurby again and after we'd left we'd only turned about four corners when we arrived at the scene of the accident, which involved two road bikes. A husband and wife from Germany had been travelling on one of the bikes while a sole rider was on the other; all three were lying motionless in the middle of the road. We were the first on the scene and stopped immediately to see if we could do anything to help. This was one of those rare times when Rob's wife Louise and my wife Gillian were with us and the first thing we did was to call for an ambulance. Sadly two died at the scene and the third person succumbed to their injuries the next day. It hit us really hard. The experience further cemented Robert's belief that riding a motorcycle on the open roads was much more dangerous than competing at high speed on closed roads: very rarely would you ever have found Robert or Joey out on a road bike.

Although I would never have dreamed of mentioning it, I always felt that if I was ever going to lose Rob to road racing then it would happen at the TT. The races are so long and the circuit is so challenging that not only does it take incredible skill and courage to compete there at the top level, but luck also plays a big part. He had had a few brushes with death on the Mountain Course before we got together and was involved in a serious accident in 1986 at the 13th Milestone, suffering a catalogue of injuries including a punctured lung, broken ribs and a broken shoulder blade, cheek and jaw. He lost the front end and I feel it was due to a second-hand tyre he had purchased, which had buckled under the pressure at high speed as he entered the corner. It was a terrible accident and Rob had a lot of internal bleeding as a result, which the doctors were having difficulty stopping. It was so serious that the doctors recommended that his family be warned that the worst could happen. As Rob battled his injuries in hospital Joey contacted a faith healer that he had great belief in and, to everyone's amazement, Rob's internal bleeding stopped and he pulled through.

On another occasion, in 1993, Rob was really flying on the 250cc Yamaha on the final night of practice on the Friday before race week and reckoned he was close to lap-record pace; he could tell the bike was performing at a high level and he was in the zone himself, man and machine in perfect harmony. He ventured out again and a while later I received the dreaded call over the loudspeaker – that I should report to Mrs Armes at the TT's Race Incident Office. My heart sank because I instinctively knew that Rob had come off somewhere and as I made my way to the office I saw Joey pulling in down the pit lane. He dumped the bike and came running up to me, saying, 'Robert's off, but he's okay. They've taken him to Noble's Hospital in the helicopter.' Joey explained that the chain had broken and jammed in the back wheel at the Waterworks but said Rob was sitting up and talking, which was very reassuring to hear. I reported to Mrs Armes anyway and she repeated what Joey had already told me.

I jumped into the van and drove over to Noble's Hospital. When I was shown in to see Rob he was in much worse shape than I'd expected. He had sustained a dislocation in the area of his pelvis and hips and was in terrible pain; he'd injured himself in the same area before and it seemed to be worse this time around. There was another rider, to Robert's left in the ward, who had also been involved in a crash that day and the little finger on his left hand was hanging on by the proverbial thread. He was shouting at the doctors, 'Take it off, take it off,' because the first race was taking place the next day and he didn't want to miss it. I found out that this particular rider had landed over Ballaugh Bridge and run into another rider in front of him, whose machine had slowed suddenly. The guy behind tried to take evasive action but somehow his hand became tangled in the exhaust of the bike in front of him and his finger was all but ripped off his hand. The doctor who was tending to Robert leaned across and whispered to me, 'Are they all as mad as he is?' Robert was pleading with the doctor to allow him to leave and somehow we managed to get him to agree, though I had to catch Rob when he tried to stand up. He was as white as a sheet with the pain and I put him on to my back and carried him out to the van; he was tremendously brave, tougher in that respect than anyone I have ever known. Robert was desperately keen to race, that year especially, because it was his chance to ride the Oxford Products Ducati, and he hated to let people down. And the Isle of the Man TT is undoubtedly the Blue Riband event in the road racing season, and the racers are building up to it the whole year.

I knew that Rob hadn't eaten much that day so we drove down to a wee restaurant near the harbour on Douglas promenade. He reluctantly agreed that he should eat but he simply couldn't walk, so when we got there I once again hoisted him on to my back and carried him inside. When we went in Steve Hislop, the great TT rider, was there with his team having a bite to eat. Steve quickly jumped up and cleared a path for us as we headed to an empty table. Rob was totally exhausted and I hated seeing him suffer like this because to me he was more like a younger brother than a friend. I ordered some pasta and chicken for him – I knew the protein would give him a boost, even if his stomach was churning at the thought of it.

It was a trying day but we'd managed to get through it and

now our thoughts turned to the Formula 1 race the next day, when Rob was contracted to ride the Oxford Products Ducati. Along with Ulsterman Mark Farmer he was part of a two-man line-up for the English team, and although I knew Rob was desperate to make a big impression on the Ducati, I couldn't see how he would be in any shape to race. We left the restaurant, and as we made our way to the hotel Robert expressed his concerns that the boss of the team would see him and pull him out of the race. I lifted him on to my back again and we hurried across the car park at the hotel – but then we heard an upstairs window being opened and, sure enough, out popped the head of the team manager. He shouted down, 'Well Liam, how is he? Is he in bed?' The car park was dimly lit and it was obvious he didn't see Robert hanging on to my back, so I played along and told him, 'Aye, he's not too bad, I'm just back from checking on him.' Needless to say he wasn't a fan of the two-strokes and he hollered back, 'What did I tell you about those bloody two-strokes? They're death traps.' For the record, this guy was another one who fell into that bracket of what I would deem the classic asshole and I just nodded back at him as I tried to keep Rob out of view. I got Robert up to his room and sat him down on the bed and I arranged to call in with him the next morning at around seven o'clock to check if he was able to race. It was part of his deal with the Oxford Products Ducati team that Rob stayed in their hotel so on this occasion at the TT he and I were using different accommodation.

The next morning, I hurried to Robert's hotel and went straight up to his room. He was still in bed and barely able to move. 'That's it, Rob,' I said. 'There's no way you can ride a Superbike for six laps round this place.' He was having none of it though and suggested he might be fine after a hot bath. He had a huge chance to catch the eye of the bigger teams with a strong ride in the Formula One race that day and was loath to give it up. In these situations all I could do was offer my advice

– the final decision on whether or not he competed lay with Robert himself. Once he made his mind up, I backed him 100 per cent, whether or not I agreed with him. I ran him a hot bath and lifted him into the tub and then headed outside to the hotel's workshops, where the Oxford Products team members and bikes were, along with a couple of guys from the press. All eyes focused on me as they sought my opinion on whether or not Robert was fit enough to compete in the Formula One race, which was a matter of a few hours away. 'I'll let Robert answer that in about fifteen minutes' time,' I replied.

Shortly after I went back up to Robert's room and helped him get dried after his bath. I still had to carry him down the stairs and out into the garage where the team was waiting. I had asked the two guys from the press to leave the garage before I went to fetch Rob and when I walked in I'll never forget the look on the team's faces as I carried Robert over and set him on to his bike. He gingerly leant forward and took hold of the handlebars in the crouched racing position. Then, after a few moments, he gave the nod of approval, looked up and said, 'I'm okay to go.' I kept my views to myself but as soon as we went back to Rob's hotel room I told him it was madness. We reached a bit of a compromise, agreeing that if he felt he was too sore to carry on or if it was to dangerous, then he'd give me the sign during the first pit stop and I'd get him off the bike. I knew Robert didn't want to let the team down and so we headed to the paddock to prepare for the race. When the time arrived, Rob donned the blue and white Oxford Products Ducati leathers and bravely tried to disguise his pain as he hobbled over to the bike on the Glencrutchery Road. I tried to force a smile as I walked alongside him but inwardly my stomach was in knots. I love the sport of road racing, but not to the extent where I was comfortable watching someone taking risks over and above the dangers that were already present in normal circumstances. We knew that the adrenaline would serve as a natural painkiller to a degree, as soon as the flag dropped, but my concern was that Rob's split-second reactions could be affected by his injuries. He accelerated off the line, clicking through the gears as he rapidly gathered momentum on the big Ducati before taking the plunge down Bray Hill; in a few seconds he was gone and I made the lonely walk back to the paddock. I went to the Hailwood Centre for a cup of tea and it offered the chance to get rid of some of the nerves because I could have a chat with some of the other mechanics and team members in there. This time, though, I made my way back to the Oxford Products pit box long before Robert was due back and the team were well prepared for his arrival, oblivious to the possibility that his race could be over when he made his scheduled stop. We had decided before not to let the team know that Rob might call it quits after the first two laps in case it affected their groundwork: we didn't want them taking their eye off the ball in case Robert was able to continue. Robert's light lit up to indicate that he had reached Signpost corner, which was only a couple of miles away. I thanked the man above, because I knew that my man was almost home, even if he had only completed one third of the race distance.

He pulled into the pits and immediately signalled to me that his race was over. I shouted, 'Stop!' and lifted Rob off the bike – the team looked at me as though I had lost the plot. I escorted Rob across the paddock to the van and I almost knocked over Geoff Cannell, the revered TT commentator, as he attempted to grab an interview. Geoff was a legend with the roving microphone in gasoline alley and I had to apologise to him afterwards – it's just that neither Rob nor I were in a talkative mood at that point. The fact that Robert had to pull out of the race didn't go down too well with the Oxford Products hierarchy. They said little about it, but it had previously been conveyed to us that they were unhappy with Robert riding two-stroke machines in the 125cc and 250cc classes. They had assumed that an engine seizure was the most likely cause of Rob's accident – quite a common problem with the two-stroke machines – but on this occasion the chain had actually snapped and wrapped itself around the swinging arm, causing the rear wheel to lock up. It had snapped when Robert had exited Ramsey Hairpin and was driving hard up towards Waterworks. I travelled out to the scene of the incident and there was still a big black tyre mark in the road, which had been caused when the back wheel had locked. Later, when Rob was feeling a bit more like his old self, he told me he had made a somewhat unwanted discovery as a result of his accident at Waterworks: 'LB, you know that lovely big laurel hedge we're always admiring at the Waterworks? Well, there's a two-foot stone wall directly in behind it.' This was typical of Robert's luck. Even Joey remarked to me that every time Rob crashed, he managed to hit something hard. The Oxford Products deal quickly petered out after Robert's crash but I certainly didn't lose much sleep over it because I found most of those involved to be obnoxious and pompous. I wouldn't tar every person in the Oxford Products set-up with that particular brush, but those who were higher up the ladder fell wholly into that category.

Ten
Crashing out

Robert's crash during practice on the 250cc Yamaha in 1993 was a nasty one, but worse was to come the following year, much worse in fact. That season Rob was riding for the Medd Honda team on the new RC45 machine, and all the guys in the outfit were a terrific bunch to work with. The Medd brothers, Stuart, Nick and John, were extremely professional but also down to earth, normal guys. They were wealthy, yes, but they'd come up the hard way and knew fine well what a bowl of porridge looked like. The whole Medd team absolutely loved Robert and he enjoyed riding for them.

That fateful season had began positively as Robert gained some strong results in the British Supercup Championship before notching up a superb double in the Superbike class at the North West 200. His performances fuelled everyone's hopes and expectations ahead of the TT and we arrived on the island full of optimism. The Medd Honda RC45 had so far proved fast and reliable and Robert was in excellent form going into the most important road race of the season. He was improving all the time on the bigger capacity machines and gaining a reputation as a serious contender on the four-strokes, adding to his already proven capabilities on the smaller two-stroke bikes. As usual I was working away in Robert's pit box when the Formula One race roared into life: my role was to observe the preparation for his scheduled stops for fuel and tyres, and to ensure that everyone making a contribution remained calm and focused. The race was held on a Sunday that year – it was postponed after two laps on the Saturday due to heavy rain and poor visibility on the Mountain section. Steve Hislop had set the pace on the Castrol Honda Britain RC45, leading team-mate Phillip McCallen by almost twenty-two seconds at the end of the opening lap, with Robert holding third place. Robert arrived in for his pit stop and the team did a marvellous job, sticking to the strategy of staying calm, working collectively and performing each task competently. The big Honda snarled into life once more and Robert was soon revving up through the gears as he exited gasoline alley and prepared for the plunge down Bray Hill with a full tank of fuel. Not long afterwards, word reached us that he had come off just after the famous Ballaugh Bridge part of the circuit, some seventeen miles out. The accident had happened on the fourth lap of the scheduled six-lap race and at first I was confused as to what exactly could have gone wrong, because the exit of Ballaugh Bridge isn't a typical crash black spot on the TT course.

As per usual, my name was announced over the loudspeaker, summoning me to report to Mrs Armes at the Race Incident Office, exploding that stomach-churning feeling of dread inside me. I had reached the office almost before the announcement had ended and I could tell straight away by the expression on Mrs Armes' face that it was serious. The alarm bells inside my head began to ring much more loudly when she said, 'You'd better come in Liam.' Any other time that Robert had been involved in a crash, Mrs Armes had relayed the message through the open hatch at the front of the office, so I knew now that my worst fears had become a reality. I braced myself for what I knew could only be bad news as an emotional Mrs Armes informed me, 'It's not good this time, Liam. Robert has sustained very serious injuries. He is unconscious and is being transferred to Noble's Hospital by helicopter. Off you go quickly and I'll say a prayer.' I was trying to keep my composure but inwardly I was close to hysterical and, once I reached the solace of our van to begin making my way to the hospital, I broke down in tears. I knew that this crash was different and while I was trying to hope for the best, deep down I was expecting the worst. As I approached the entrance to Noble's the helicopter with Robert on board was just about to land. I bolted into reception; my head was spinning and I desperately craved some crumb of comfort, news that perhaps Robert would be okay. I was simply told to take a seat and, before I knew it, the foyer of the hospital began to fill up with concerned family and friends. Robert's father Willie was there, plus his brothers Jim and Joey, and then later, once the news had began to filter out, members of the press started to arrive. Everything was happening in a blur and after some time had passed the doctor approached us and asked for Robert's immediate family.

Willie stepped forward and the doctor asked him to nominate three family members to go and see Rob in the trauma room before he was taken to theatre. I genuinely felt the doctor was of the opinion that we would be saying our final goodbyes to Robert, such was the severity of his injuries. Willie put forward Joey, Jim and me, and the three of us were quickly ushered up the corridor towards what I assumed to be the trauma room, which resembled a theatre, where Robert was being treated.

We went inside and were greeted by a distressing sight: Robert was lying comatose on the bed with an oxygen mask over his face, and lots of doctors rushing around frantically, working feverishly in an effort to save his life. I will never forget the pool of blood lying below Robert and what shocked me in particular was how thick it was; almost like red mercury. It's an image I'll never be able to erase from my mind for the rest of my days. Jim, Joey and I just stood there, frozen to the spot, unable to speak and in a complete state of shock. Never had Robert looked so badly broken and it was all I could do to stop myself from welling up. After what seemed like an eternity but was probably only a matter of a few minutes, Joey turned to me and said, 'Liam, I think he's trying to say something to you.' Sure enough, I could see Rob was trying to speak through the oxygen mask and I leaned in towards him and told him not to try and talk, to rest himself. However, the doctor said it was okay for him to try to speak and lifted up his oxygen mask, so I put my ear closer to his mouth in an effort to hear his voice, which, understandably, was barely a whisper. I was astonished when he murmured, 'The back wheel came off her, LB, the back wheel came off.' With that, we were guided out of the room and Jim began crying very sore, realising that his brother's life was hanging by a thread. He went to pieces and some staff members came along and escorted us to a private room, well away from any prying eyes and the press. It was an awful scenario, but looking back now the staff at Noble's were absolutely wonderful and I have to make special mention of their professionalism and the manner in which they looked after us and – of course – all that they did for Robert.

After an hour or so, one of the hospital staff informed us that the operation was likely to be a long, drawn-out affair and Joey – still wearing his racing leathers with a jacket pulled over the top – Jim and their father Willie decided to head back to the places they were staying. The Dunlop family is a very tight-knit unit and they must have felt that this was the best way for them to deal with the fact that Robert was fighting for his life against very steep odds. They were each fighting to hold back the tears, as was I, and I felt that they would prefer to try and come to terms with their emotions in privacy, away from the confines of the hospital. At times such as this the Dunlops much prefer their own company, seeking comfort from within. They also knew that I would keep them informed of any developments by telephone. I remained behind and was told that Robert would be in theatre for around two hours. This was around five o'clock that evening and some three hours later I received an update that it was now likely Rob would remain in the theatre until around ten o'clock that night. More hours came and passed and eventually, at around half past eleven, I was told he was finally out and had been taken to a high dependency unit.

I was asked to report to the surgeon's office for a briefing on Robert's condition. I'll never forget that meeting as the surgeon was still wearing a blood-soaked shirt with his tie tucked into a gap between the buttons at the top. He looked visibly shattered, as I was also, and both of us were decidedly irritable. I wanted answers and perhaps I was looking for someone to blame, while he wasn't exactly in conversational mood. He did give me a step-by-step breakdown of Robert's injuries, explaining that he had suffered life-threatening wounds to his right-hand side in particular, caused – it later transpired – when Robert slammed into a brick wall at around 140mph. Robert's right arm and leg were badly mangled, and the surgeon told me that while they were working to save his arm in theatre, his leg had begun to turn black, indicating gangrene, and they immediately focused their efforts on addressing that problem, to stave off the threat of amputation. But as they treated Robert's leg, the same problem developed with his arm, which had also started to turn black. Incredibly and by the grace of God, Rob still had two arms and two legs as we spoke, and that revelation came as a massive relief.

It proved to be only a brief flicker of light in the darkness, however, and the wind soon left my sails when I learned that all the nerves in Robert's right arm and leg had been severed. Additionally, I was warned that the ensuing forty-eight hours would be critical to his prospects of recovery. I was left in no doubt that Rob's life was in grave danger as a result of the trauma his body had sustained in the accident. It had been a long and emotionally draining night and I was utterly distraught. Robert was fighting for his life and there wasn't a thing I could do to help him. This was one battle he was going to have to win on his own. I was given permission to go and see him again in the high dependency unit and when I got there, I realised that he was sharing the unit with two other competitors, one suffering from severe head injuries and the other on a life support machine – he was an organ donor who was being kept alive until a suitable recipient could be found. It quickly dawned on me that, despite Robert's precarious situation, he was actually the most fortunate of the three in there, and that offered me a small ray of hope.

Rob was heavily sedated and I took a chair beside him, rubbing his lips with ice cubes throughout the night. His shattered arm and leg were wrapped in bandages and in traction, yet the blood still seeped out from his wounds, dropping on to an absorbent pad underneath. There was an eerie silence in the unit, except for the electronic bleeps from the lifesaving equipment, and it was a long and dismal night. I prayed, God knows I prayed that he would pull through, but I felt guilty pleading with the Lord to spare him because I wasn't what you would call a regular churchgoer – far from it, in fact.

After I had been to see him, I left the hospital and returned to my hotel in Douglas to pick up some toiletries and a change of clothes. It was the early hours of the morning but I had promised Joey I would call with him at his cottage at Groudle Glen. As his wife Linda made us a cup of tea, I brought Joey up to speed with the latest news from the hospital. Joey didn't say much – he never did – but he was devastated. Over the next few days, I spent almost all my time at Robert's bedside and when Joey, Jim and Willie called at the hospital, normally when things were quieter, I went to meet them in the tearoom and made sure they knew of any changes in Rob's condition. The following day, the news that Robert's rear wheel had been defective began to become more widespread, with details emerging that it had somehow broken up at high speed, leaving Rob with no chance and causing him a catalogue of horrendous injuries.

The fact that the wheel had broken apart almost defied belief. This led to the organisers of that year's TT checking all wheels of a similar nature. They found several more that were defective, and had to be replaced. In some ways, it was comforting to know that Robert's accident had saved others from a similar disaster. In the end, some years later, it was proved beyond all doubt that the wheel was defective, and Robert finally won his case and received compensation.

That would all come later – right now all that mattered was Robert's life. The motorcycling community rallies around at times like these and I must mention Brian Kreisky, who owned several companies producing motorsport videos and live race coverage that he syndicated around the world. Brian came to the hospital and told me that there was a plane waiting at Ronaldsway Airport to take me back home to Northern Ireland at any time to see my family or indeed to collect any of Robert's family and fly them over to be with him. He always got on well with us and it was a fantastic gesture; I never forgot him for that. In the aftermath of Robert's accident, it was actually Brian who sourced the now infamous amateur video footage that captured the moment the rear wheel of Robert's Medd Honda disintegrated. He also pledged to steer us in the direction of good lawyers to take up Robert's case if he survived. There were many in the media, like Jackie Fullerton, Mark Robson, Stephen Watson and Terry Smyth, who also gave their support, whether calling at the hospital or phoning to check on Robert's progress and offer words of comfort.

I became friends with the family of the injured rider who was being kept alive on the ventilator and I was heartbroken for them when one night it became clear that a recipient for the organs had been found. For his family, it was over and I embraced them in the corridor. In that instant the stark reality of the risks taken by every road racer and the consequences of what can happen when things go wrong really hit home hard. I was bearing witness to the ugly side of the sport; the life-ending impact it can have on the competitors in a split second, and the devastation left behind for their families.

Rob's time in hospital was a very sobering experience, but there were one or two occasions when I managed a little smile, especially when a fairly large nurse came over to Rob's bedside and offered me a cup of tea. I gladly accepted, and then she told me she had volunteered for overtime because she wanted to be around to help Robert on his road to recovery, admitting that she thought he was 'absolutely gorgeous'. As we stood there looking at him lying there, out for the count and none the wiser, I said, 'You know what, you're right. He is a handsome wee bugger.'

Over the next few days Robert gradually began to respond to treatment and was eased out of sedation to the point where he was able to communicate. Now that he was more with it and able to hold a conversation, I told him that I had some good news and some bad news. 'Give me the good news first, LB,' Rob said. So I dutifully enlightened him that one of the nurses had taken a strong fancy to him. 'Is that true? Which one?' he asked, no doubt having noticed that quite a few of them were very easy on the eye. 'Well, that's the bad news,' I told him. I could see his eyes scanning around the ward until he caught sight of the big, hefty one and then he exclaimed, 'Aw naw, LB!' It was a clear sign that Robert was finally on the mend and he actually began to laugh quietly, forcing his traction to move around to the extent where I had to stop him before he did himself more serious damage. The get well soon cards were beginning to pile up and the mood all around was decidedly much brighter. The darkness had lifted and the aim now was to get Rob back home to Northern Ireland before we began to assess what the future might hold for him. His injuries were so severe that his career in road racing at that juncture was, to all intents and purposes, finished. The doctor had been pretty accurate in his summary of Robert's injuries on the night of the crash. All the nerves in Rob's right arm and leg were severed, leaving him with a 'drop' foot and hand and badly hampering his movement. I tried my hardest to appear as optimistic as possible in front of him but, in reality, I was gutted because I suspected that one of Ireland's greatest ever motorcycle racers had been cruelly robbed of his chance to go on to bigger and better things, through absolutely no fault of his own. After a number of weeks, the medical experts decided that Robert was well enough to be transferred home. He then spent some time at the Ulster Hospital, and so began the long road to recovery.

Eleven
Hardy breed

While Robert was recovering we continued to attend motorcycle races, and the Medd Honda team even arranged for us to fly over to attend the Race of Champions at Mallory Park as their guests. So many people were unstinting in their generosity towards us, but it was no substitute whatsoever for the satisfaction or the buzz we got from being involved in the highly charged and competitive environment of motorcycle road racing, especially for Rob. We actually returned to the Isle of Man in 1995, one year on from Robert's crash, and thanked countless friends for the support they had shown only twelve months earlier when Rob had literally been at death's door. Although Rob was thankful to be alive, it was clear to me that he was still extremely frustrated at not being able to get out there and race.

We also both attended the Ulster Grand Prix as spectators in 1995 and it was incredible to see his reaction as we watched the action from the end of the Flying Kilo — a long straight that includes the finish line where riders reach speeds of around 190mph. It actually scared the hell out of Robert and this was someone who was usually on the bike, scaring the hell out of the spectators. He decided it was time to move on and we ended up at a famous part of the 7.4-mile course known as the Deer's Leap – a rollercoaster-like downhill plunge where the front wheel snaps skywards as competitors drop down towards the tree-lined Cochranstown section well in excess of 150mph. Again, Robert was taken aback by the sheer speed of his fellow racers – perhaps watching from the side of the road brought it home to him how frighteningly quick it all seemed from a static position. We ventured down towards Cochranstown for a race or two and then onwards as far as the Flowbog Crossroads before Rob decided he'd seen enough. We made our move in between the races and headed for home. It was amazing how someone like Robert, himself one of the fastest men out there, found it uncomfortable to watch the racing. He clearly felt much more at home on the bike than in the hedgerows.

It was a difficult time and a cloud of uncertainty engulfed Robert in relation to the options available to him. The grip level in his right hand was strictly limited and, while he could grasp an item the size of a can of baked beans and hold it reasonably tightly, he had virtually zero grip when it came to holding something smaller like a pencil. The idea of returning to his career as a road racer seemed impossible, but just like each time before, once the broken bones began to mend, that flicker of desire to get back on a motorcycle began to grow stronger. Any thoughts Robert may have harboured about retiring for good were gone and one evening that indomitable spirit that the Dunlops are renowned for was perfectly encapsulated when his father Willie and mum May arrived at my door. Willie was carrying a crude prototype glove engineered in the unique Dunlop way that he hoped my mother-in-law, who was a dressmaker by trade, could make more presentable. The glove was an invention aimed at enabling Robert to overcome the grip deficit in his right hand; that would hopefully allow him to grip the throttle of a motorcycle once more. A small spring was attached to the glove behind each finger, with the idea that each time Robert closed his hand as best he could to grip the throttle, the springs would compress. When he relaxed his grip, they would recoil, automatically straightening out his fingers and creating a extra dimension to the movement in his hand. It was crude, but it started us down the road of making modifications that would enable Robert to race again.

Robert had faced challenging situations in the past after accidents but the task that lay before him this time was unprecedented. He was permanently disabled by his injuries and it seemed there was no way he would ever be able to compete on a conventional motorcycle again. For a start, he had lost the ability to use the front brake lever – located on the right-hand side of a motorcycle on the throttle – and even holding on to the handlebars would be next to impossible. The only positive was that his ability to use the gear change with his left foot was unaffected, and although the rear brake was operated from the right-hand side, using it wasn't an absolutely necessity, even if it did come in handy for lowering the front wheel if the bike popped a massive wheelie or for steering the bike in a slide. The challenges he faced were evident in everyday life and now that Robert was back driving again, it was plain to see the effort required to pilot a van or a car, never mind a racing motorcycle.

I still had the wee 125cc Honda in my garage and one night I took a phone call from Robert, asking if I would be at home the following day. 'I'm going to call down and tinker a bit with the wee lady.' It was then I knew for certain that Rob was going to attempt a racing comeback. I had talked to him about the need to retire until I was blue in the face. It pained me to see someone who was on the verge of world greatness, pre-1994, a mere shadow of what he used to be. Not only did I worry for his safety, but I felt he had nothing left to prove to anyone. But the more I said, the more determined he became. Once I realised he wasn't for turning, I told him I was behind him again 100 per cent. He was so determined that he would have done it with or without my help, so it was a no brainer that I would be there with him. I was also aware that Robert's wife Louise was extremely supportive of his decision because she knew what road racing meant to him.

He was like a kid at Christmas when he arrived at my house the next day and nothing would do but he had to take the bike, with a slight modification to the throttle, out for a blast up the road. He put his helmet on and fired up the bike and away he went in his jeans and a black bomber jacket. It was a straight country road and he kept his word that he wouldn't stray too far, perhaps travelling for a mile or so before turning back. I welled up as I watched him return towards me, the famous black and white Arai helmet coming into sight and Robert at the controls of a motorcycle once more. It was a poignant moment and my mind flashed back to that awful night when we went to see him in the trauma room at Noble's Hospital, when I thought I was saying goodbye for the final time. I helped him off the bike and once he had taken off his helmet I could see the unmistakeable glint in his eye: the most gifted 125cc rider ever from this island was back on the comeback trail.

Robert – who had inherited that Dunlop trait of being mechanically gifted – had managed to trace an American rider who had suffered similar serious injuries to those that now afflicted him. During the course of his research, he ascertained that the American had moved the front brake lever from the right handlebar and converted it to a thumb-operated brake on the left, right beside the clutch. It was a model he was keen to try so we enlisted the help of my uncle Jackie to install a similar thumb-operated front brake on the 125cc Honda – he was restricted to the wee lady as there was absolutely no way he could attempt to ride anything bigger given the physical limitations he faced. Even riding the 125cc was a monumental challenge and we had no idea whether or not his planned return would prove to be a success. Robert was effectively starting over and it was testament to his resolve that he was even attempting to resume racing. Prior to his accident at the TT Robert had been a world-class rider with a huge future ahead of him; he now found himself resorting to unorthodox and largely untried methods simply to ride a motorcycle once more.

After countless nights toiling away in the workshop we finally perfected a thumb-operated braking system for the front wheel and Robert did a spot of testing on the country roads around my house; it was never a problem for my neighbours because most were Dunlop fans so no one objected when we closed off the narrow lanes for an impromptu test. Robert was all the while stepping up his rehab but I still had major concerns about the path we were embarking on. I was fearful of the risks involved and worried about Robert's ability to grip the handlebar and throttle with his right hand. The surgeon who treated Robert at Noble's Hospital had explained to me that even though Robert's brain would be sending him signals that he was gripping the throttle tightly, in reality he would be barely holding on, with the damage he had suffered to his nerves in conflict with the messages he would be receiving from his brain.

The point came when Robert had undertaken sufficient rehabilitation that he felt ready to make a competitive return to racing. The press went into overdrive, with plenty of column inches devoted to the debate on whether or not the 'Mighty Micro' would ever be able to return to the heights he had previously scaled in the 125cc class. I felt very apprehensive but nothing could hold Rob back. We made several trips to Shackleton Barracks in Ballykelly in the north-west, close to the city of Londonderry, where there was a small airfield with a two-mile runway. Robert wanted to do some flat-out testing on the long, perfectly straight airstrip. Robert's brother-in-law Jim Stevenson came with us on one trip when Robert was especially keen to get up to maximum speed and hold the throttle fully open over a considerable distance to get an idea of the effects on his right hand. He asked me to take the bike for a few lengths of the straight to warm it up and I obliged, going back and forth until he waved me down. 'That's enough, LB, you're going so slow you remind me of my postman' were his exact words. Rob took over and in no time at all he was off like a bat out of hell, quickly becoming no more than a small dot on the horizon. He made a few trips up and down the runway and as he almost disappeared from view again, the unmistakeable howl of the two-stroke Honda ceased and the air fell silent. I knew Robert had come off but I was so far past myself with worry that I began to run up the runway instead of getting into the van. Jim had his wits about him, though, and took off, flying past me in the van. I could barely breathe when I got there after running the whole way and I found Jim cradling Robert in his arms, with the wee Honda lying about one hundred yards away in bits. Robert was barely conscious and it was obvious he had a badly broken arm, with part of the bone protruding through his jacket. It was a shocking sight and we quickly lifted him into the van and sped to an office within the army camp, from where an ambulance was summoned.

As Robert was transported to Altnagelvin Hospital in Londonderry, we ventured back up the runway to collect what was left of the bike. It was scarcely believable that after all Robert had been through in the aftermath of his near-death crash at the Isle of Man TT, he was now back in hospital with yet more injuries, his comeback firmly on hold and all his hard work wiped out in one fell swoop before he'd even made it back on to a racing grid. I felt terrible having to pick up the phone to ring his wife Louise and his mum May with yet more bad news. It knocked the stuffing out of us all over again and I felt sure that this would be the final message that Robert needed to convince him that his time in this sport was up. This was fate's way of telling him to hang up those scuffed and tired leathers once and for all, right? Damn the bit of it: Robert was quickly out of hospital with his arm in plaster, urging me to get the bike mended because 'this is only a wee blip, LB'. I couldn't believe my ears.

As had been the case before, Robert's broken bones mended and his resolve remained shatterproof. Nothing could prise him away from motorcycles and he simply lived for the buzz of riding at incredible speeds. He undertook a new rehabilitation programme as he plotted his return once more. The absolute determination of the man was on a level I had never seen before and I don't believe I will ever again meet someone with the same mental fortitude.

His permanently damaged right arm and foot were a cause of concern for many people in positions of authority within the organisational structure of motorcycle road races, none more so than Billy Nutt, who was the top administrator in the sport at the time and the man in charge of the North West 200. Billy had called at Robert's home on a courtesy visit and sat down at the table as Rob was eating his dinner. It became obvious to Billy that Rob was having extreme difficulty even holding a knife, and he noticed that Robert had to switch from his impaired right hand to his good left hand as he attempted to cut the meat on his dinner plate. Billy said nothing, but he returned home that night completely shocked by what he had seen. A few days later, Billy announced the bombshell news that Robert was barred from competing at the 1996 North West 200. The decision rocked the sport to its very foundations, but Billy felt Robert's injuries were too severe to enable him to compete safely.

It soon began to feel as though everyone involved in the organisation of road races was following his lead. Worse was to come when the sport's governing body, the Motorcycle Union of Ireland (MCUI), revoked Robert's licence, stating that Robert's injuries were too severe to enable him to control a racing motorcycle, and that his modified 125cc Honda was not race worthy. Many would have felt at the time that this was the end of Robert Dunlop's long-running quest to return to the big time, but in hindsight it was only the beginning. The gloves were off as far as Robert was concerned and he entered into legal battle with Billy Nutt and the motorcycling establishment. Rob's long-time sponsor, PJ O'Kane, waded in with financial support and legal experts took up his case in an effort to have the decision reversed. If we failed in our attempts, Robert's career would be over and he would never race again.

It would be possible for me to fill a book alone on what went on behind the scenes during the lengthy legal battle. It began in humiliating circumstances at the House of Sport in Belfast. At this initial meeting it was brought to the attention of our legal team that they had no legal right to be in attendance because they had failed to submit their request to be present within the stated timeframe. As a result, they were asked to leave and so we departed with our tails between our legs, embarrassed and humiliated. Of course I asked how our legal team had made such a basic blunder and no one seemed able to provide an answer; it was obvious they had made a right balls-up. They hastily concocted a Plan B, advising me that I had the right to go back in and represent Robert. Minutes later I found myself clutching a large file of documents as I was ushered through the door back into the meeting. Robert and PJ were with me, but were abruptly informed that they were forbidden from entering. It was a total shambles and Robert made sure our legal team knew it. I can remember PJ paying them off in the car park outside to dispense with their services. If it had been me, I wouldn't have given them as much as a cold penny.

A new legal team was put in place soon after and evidence was gathered from as far afield as America to back up our case that Robert's modified machine was fit for purpose. Independent medical professionals were sourced to pass judgement on Robert's injuries and analyse whether they felt he was physically and mentally capable of resuming his racing career. Our new legal team was working around the clock and soon they were ready to take on Billy Nutt and the motorcycling establishment. To our utter delight, we won – we proved that Rob was fit to race and that his Honda was not a liability. It was fabulous news, but the development wasn't met with universal approval and I recall some of Robert's rivals airing their misgivings over racing against him in the future. We won the battle, but the war continued and Billy Nutt still refused to accept Robert's entries for any of the events at which he was the clerk of the course. Two of the those meetings were the North West 200 and the Ulster Grand Prix – the two most important road races in Ireland – so Robert was gutted. I chose to blank Billy because I was firmly in Rob's corner, along with PJ O'Kane, and we certainly weren't about to throw in the towel.

A short time later and purely by chance I happened to bump into Billy smack in the middle of the main street in Coleraine, where he had an office at the time. We met head on and we both stopped and looked at each other; call it fate or whatever, but we spoke to one another, and in a pretty short space of time we agreed that we would hold a meeting with Robert at Billy's office to see if we could find any common ground and rebuild some bridges. We were adamant that the meeting between the three of us would be kept strictly private, with no press, solicitors or any other race officials present. I still had the unenviable task of selling the idea to Robert, who had made Billy Nutt his number one enemy. I had detected in Billy a willingness at least to get back on speaking terms with Rob, even if there was little chance of a change of heart. The North West 200 circuit was Robert's favourite course and I knew how desperately he wanted to return there as a competitive rider. It was ironic that I found Robert working away on the little 125cc Honda in my garage when I came home from Coleraine that day. I made some small talk for a few minutes and then informed him that I'd bumped into Billy and that perhaps the time was right for the three of us to sit down together and see if there was even the possibility of a compromise. Robert, understandably, was more than a little annoyed; in fact he nearly hit the roof. I backed off but I knew that I'd at least planted the seed and had given him something to mull over. It didn't take him long to come round to the idea − later that evening he phoned me to ask more about what Billy had said to me that day in Coleraine. He raised the subject again the following day over a cup of tea at my house and after some discussion he said, 'Okay, LB, let's go for it − tell him the meeting is on.'

It was a beautiful sunny day when we went to see Billy at his office on New Row in Coleraine. Rob picked me up, wearing his sunglasses as usual. When we arrived, Billy welcomed us in and we sat down on two chairs directly across the desk from him. Billy would later tell me that he felt that Rob had landed the first blow by wearing his sunglasses, denying Billy the opportunity to look him in the eye. It was a smart move and something we were able to laugh about later, but the tone of the meeting was deadly serious. The atmosphere was incredibly tense and I found myself almost playing the role of mediator, attempting to keep the conversation flowing even when we seemed to be getting nowhere. Yet, against unfavourable odds, the meeting proved beneficial and we left having agreed to further dialogue over our differences, which would eventually pave the way for Robert's return to the North West 200.

In the wake of the legal wrangling, the first two clubs to accept Robert's entry forms were the Cookstown 100 and Tandragee 100 respectively. I have never forgotten either club for giving Robert the opportunity to race again, and neither has the Dunlop family. Both events received plenty of criticism from those in the anti-Robert Dunlop brigade, but they stuck to their guns and Rob was thrown a lifeline as he sought to prove that he still had what it took to win races.

Robert made his racing comeback at the Cookstown 100 in April 1996. We arrived in the paddock and it was wet, which was the last thing he needed. He already had to contend with adapting to a vastly changed motorcycle and, of course, he was still struggling with his injuries. I told him to ease himself back into it and not to be embarrassed if he was well down in the field because this was merely a stepping stone on the road back. A lump grew in my throat as Rob pulled on his leathers in the back of the van – the extent of the challenges he had overcome to get to this point hit me. By hook or by crook, he was back doing what he loved: Robert Dunlop was racing again. He finished in an uncustomary ninth place, but this race wasn't about getting a result and he returned safely in one piece. I must admit he did look awkward out there, but it wasn't really a surprise given the circumstances. It felt like a bit of an anti-climax, but Robert was undeterred and pulled up at my house the next morning to strip the machine down in preparation for the Tandragee 100, which was the next race on the calendar the following weekend. He was like an excited schoolboy all over again and was determined to improve on his comeback result at Tandragee, although the newly fitted thumb-operated front brake was posing more problems than we had anticipated. Robert was slowly getting used to it but it was causing him severe cramps in his left forearm, which was creating pain in his arm, wrist and hand. The issue was that he was using muscles that had never really been used before. As a result, Robert resorted to putting his arm, his good arm as we called it, up behind his back when he had time for a short breather on a straight section of the circuit during a race to flex his fingers in order to ease the cramps. It meant that he was only holding on to his machine with one arm, his damaged right arm, and it was a major worry for me. The throttle on the right-hand twist grip of the bike had also been modified, ensuring there was a shorter movement from closed to fully open as Robert's wrist had very limited movement. Even with the alteration, Rob quite often had to do a double grab in order to hold the throttle fully open and he also found that he had to hold his right arm at a protruding right angle so he could operate the throttle, which meant his riding style had changed dramatically.

It wasn't easy for Rob. In 1997, the first year that he was back racing at the TT after his accident, he came in from practice with the colour completely drained from his face. I knew right away that he'd had a moment out on the track. As usual, I held back and didn't mention it until later in the evening, once we'd had our tea. I had been mindful that the surgeon at Noble's had told me that, because the nerves in Robert's right arm had been severed, he could have the impression that he was gripping something firmly when he might only have been holding on to it lightly. This was exactly what had happened. Rob confided in me that he'd had a hell of a shock as he was coming down the Mountain section of the course. His hand had slipped off the handlebar at very high speed, causing him to almost lose control. By the grace of God he had managed to avoid a catastrophe but my heart sank because I knew he'd had an extremely lucky escape and I was worried that he would not be so lucky the next time.

I knew Rob had been badly shook up by the incident so the next morning I let him have a lie-in and I headed down to our garage on my own and began stripping the wee Honda. About an hour later Robert arrived, carrying a brown paper bag from which he produced a cheese grater, a tapered cylindrical one. I jokily asked him if we were having a salad for tea that night but he just lifted a pair of tin snips and began to cut through the middle of the grater. Once he had cut a strip out, he proceeded to bend it around the right handlebar grip, with the pointy, razor-like indentations facing upwards. 'What are you at?' I enquired. Rob explained that he intended to secure the strip of metal cheese grater to the right twist grip with lacing wire in order to guard against his hand slipping off the throttle again. I was stunned. It was the most bizarre idea that he'd ever come up with. This improvisation seemed ludicrous to me – for a start, we had to somehow get the contraption through scrutineering. Robert, though, had already thought of that, telling me, 'We'll stick a piece of foam over both grips the same as the Grand Prix riders do to protect against greasy or oily hands and then we'll rip them off before I set off.' After much persuasion, I agreed that we could go ahead with this, but I was sick at the thought of it. The bike passed scrutineering with flying colours and I parked it up in the holding area one hour before the starting time, which was standard procedure. My stomach was churning – lots of people came over to have a look at Robert's bike but of course no one realised that we had fitted a piece of cheese grater over the right twist grip. The time soon came for Rob to fire the bike up and proceed on to the Glencrutchery Road. Robert's plan had worked. I quickly and discreetly removed the foam cover before he set off, with Rob swiftly placing his hand on the grip as soon as I had removed the foam, to guard against prying eyes. When the flag dropped and he blasted away down towards Bray Hill, I made my way to the Hailwood Centre in the paddock for a cup of tea, feeling slightly ill and at odds with my conscience. If I hadn't helped Rob, he'd have done it himself anyway and I consoled myself with the fact that it would offer him a little extra safety after the near miss in practice. I was still worried, though, because if Robert did fall off, how would I ever explain away the cheese grater and my role in covering for him? Thankfully, my man returned safely home and before anyone could say 'well done Robert' I had the offending piece of metal concealed in my jacket pocket. Yet again a piece of infamous Dunlop improvisation had succeeded. The wee man's brainwave, although ingenious, did lead me to question my sanity – I had to be mad to be involved in this desperate measure to enable Robert to race a motorcycle.

Rob's style on the bike changed dramatically after his TT crash and his physical limitations meant he was no longer the tidiest, neatest rider I have ever seen on a 125. He used to have everything tucked in on the little bike: he was almost invisible behind the screen in an effort to gain every aerodynamic advantage possible. This was essential on the wee two-strokes in order to gain maximum speed from the much less powerful engines. Now, his right elbow stuck out from the side of the fairing like a hen's broken wing, but Robert had to ride like this because he needed to use his hand for leverage to twist the throttle, since his wrist movement and hand had been rendered pretty useless due to the injuries he sustained. The king of the North West 200 was a mere shadow of the rider who had upheld Ulster pride against the overseas challengers in the past and those glory days were never to return. It was desperately sad, but Robert simply got on with it and was determined to return to winning ways nonetheless. Despite his reduced physical capabilities and the fact that he had to race with a modified thumb brake operated by his left thumb, Robert believed that he could overcome those drawbacks and experience the sweet taste of success once more at the majors.

Rob had encountered more than his fair share of misfortune during this period in his career – and it wasn't over just yet. He had finally been permitted to race again at the North West 200 in 1998, for the first time in four years, but his return didn't go to plan. Robert, who previously had up to five chances to win at each North West 200 across a variety of classes, was now limited to only one race on the wee lady; it didn't seem fair, but that's road racing. Incredibly, he was among the leading riders as they braked for University Corner at the end of the fast straight from Station Corner, preparing to tip in to the left-hander at the foot of the hill leading up towards the 'Magic' Roundabout. As the riders jostled for position, a gap appeared and David Lemon – a competent two-stroke rider – attempted to try and dive up Robert's outside. Under normal circumstances the pass would have been successful, but with Robert's right arm sticking out from the side of his machine, there was less room for close-quarters overtaking. Disaster struck as Lemon clipped Rob's arm on his way past. Robert went down heavily and it was a nasty crash captured by the television cameras at the scene. Although he was quite badly injured, it could have been much worse as the crash happened at fairly high speed even though the riders were braking down for University. The footage of the incident doesn't make for easy viewing and when I've watched the slow motion replays in the past I've often thought it could so easily have proved fatal. However, neither Robert nor I ever attributed any blame for the accident to David because it was a freak crash. David was one of the sport's gentlemen and he is still a dear friend of mine today. He visited me afterwards and was distraught about what had happened. Everyone involved in racing was aware of Robert's situation and all he had been through, and now he found himself back in hospital again after working so hard to return to the North West. I quickly assured David that no one blamed him and that put him at ease, even if it was clear he felt awful over what had occurred.

Inevitably, the incident was seized upon by those in the anti-Robert Dunlop brigade, who jumped at the opportunity to question whether or not he was still capable of racing safely. Of course Robert had actually been banned by the Clerk of the Course Billy Nutt from competing at the North West previously, and this unfortunate incident only served to stir the pot again, with some claiming he was a liability; an accident waiting to happen. Robert, though, had been through so much to get back on a bike and there was no way he was going to throw in the towel after his latest demoralising setback – such was the tenacity and defiance of the most remarkable and toughest sportsman I have ever encountered.

It was a long and hard road back to the top but Rob's ability soon shone through again. Undoubtedly his greatest success after his infamous TT crash came at the very same event in 1998 as he returned to the top of the podium, winning the Ultra Lightweight Race and confounding those who had said he would never race again, never mind win. He had finished third in the same race on his TT return the previous year but now Robert was truly back and he won in some style. As he exited Governor's Dip and appeared on the Glencrutchery Road on the last lap my heart was thumping in my chest and the tears had gathered behind my eyes. Robert took the chequered flag once again at the Isle of Man TT, four years after that terrible night when we had converged at Noble's Hospital, fearing the worst. I had chosen a relatively quiet position in gasoline alley because I felt I would crumble like a sandcastle when he finally crossed the line and, sure enough, I burst into tears. I was standing there bawling like a kid when I felt a tap on the shoulder. It was Joey's manager, Davy Wood, who said, 'Don't be embarrassed, Liam. Let it all out son.' Davy was always there with a helping hand whenever it was needed most and, unsurprisingly, when I turned around to thank him, the tears were also streaming down his face. He was a genuine friend and a genuine man, who always had the best interests of the riders at heart. Davy spent a small lifetime helping others and was always at the heart of everything good in the sport.

As I made my way down through the hordes of people to go and meet Robert, there wasn't a dry eye in the house. Even the seasoned TV, radio and press men were shedding bucket loads: Jackie Fullerton, Mark Robson and Terry Smyth and many others from BBC and Ulster Television were all putting their handkerchiefs to good use. The motorcycle road racing family were united in acknowledgement of the magnitude of the difficulties that Robert had overcome. Not only was he back racing, he was back on the top of the podium at the Isle of Man TT. As Robert stood there on the rostrum soaking up the moment I couldn't help remembering the surgeon telling me that, even if Rob somehow managed to pull through, he would never race a motorcycle again. I don't think the surgeon would have ever have believed that this victory would happen, but for me it was living proof that you should never underestimate a Dunlop.

We enjoyed a superb celebration that evening and for me it didn't get any better than that. Following any Dunlop win, both teams headed out to celebrate. A close friend who was always welcome in our company was Ireland's leading country and western star Brian Coll. He was a Dunlop man through and through and was one of the chosen few who had the opportunity to listen in to the post-race discussions. That night we embarked on a mini pub crawl of sorts. This particular night I took my fair share of pints as I tried to keep up with Robert, who – for one so small – could certainly put them away. When I'd decided that I'd had enough – I was beginning to talk like a washing machine – I said goodnight to Robert and made my way back to our accommodation on Broadway. Rob was still reasonably sober and remained behind with some close friends who had joined us during the course of the evening. As fate would have it, when I finally staggered back to our digs I discovered that I'd forgotten my keys and, as it was late, I was loath to ring the doorbell. I made my way around the back entry and climbed over the wall into the yard at the rear. I was trying to be as quiet as a mouse, but in reality I was stumbling around like an elephant. I always left our back window open as my uncle Jackie had a terrible habit of frequently breaking wind, night and day. The problem I faced was that our room was one storey up from ground level. As luck would have it, there was a sloped lean-to roof, which ran almost to the height of the open window in our room. I pulled some dustbins together to give myself leverage to get on to the roof and safely manoeuvred myself to a position directly below our window, which was still about a metre higher. In sobriety, the leap to the window would have been no problem but I found myself almost frozen to the spot as I weighed up the situation. Suddenly, the back door opened and Reg's wife June, our landlady, appeared below me. 'Liam, what the hell are you at? Come down for God's sake before you fall,' she yelled. 'You're like the man from the Milk Tray advert.' She was right too, because I was all dressed in black. I guess I should've said, 'All because the lady loves ...' I didn't live that down for a long time and Robert especially took great delight in the story when he found out.

Twelve

The wean returns the favour

I could count on the fingers of one hand the number of times Robert fell off his racing motorcycle due to a mistake made by him. Yet I've almost lost count of the number of times he ended up in hospital as a result of motorcycle road racing injuries. Robert was the unluckiest road racer I've ever known. Practically every time he came off it was either as a result of a component failure or indeed as a result of someone else taking him down. But there was one occasion in September 1998 when the roles were reversed and, instead of me gathering Robert up in a heap and transporting him off to hospital, it was the other way around. In fact there is absolutely no doubt in my mind that he saved my life that day.

It all began when Robert and I agreed to go paragliding in support of Children in Need. It was arranged that we would do a practice run one Sunday morning at Benone Strand on the north coast. Robert used always to call into my house on a Sunday morning for a few cups of tea and a few slices of a cake we loved called a ginger slab. My wife Gillian always made sure that a fresh one was there for us every Sunday morning and, believe me, very little remained of it when Rob and I had the big knife out. The Sunday morning of our planned paraglide rehearsal was no different to any other; in fact, the only difference was the weather, which was horrendously windy. The radio had said that the tail-end of a tornado was currently hitting the north-west region of Northern Ireland, the exact location of our planned parachute jump. I can remember Gillian saying to me, 'There is no way anyone with any sense will let you and Rob do that paraglide today. It would be crazy.' I told her not to worry; that we'd leave the decision up to the experts.

Then, around 8 a.m., Robert pulled into my yard in his jeep. We weren't due at Benone until ten, but we had the ginger slab cake to dismantle first. Robert had his youngest son Michael with him – he's the youngest of Rob's three sons, and Rob used to take him everywhere with him. As we looked out of my front window that morning, a weeping cherry tree was practically bent over double, such was the ferocity of the wind. 'They'll hardly put us up in that,' I said to Robert, who informed me that the experts in charge were to ring him to let him know what was happening. No sooner had Rob told me this than his phone rang, and we heard that the paragliding was on. The three of us bailed in to Robert's jeep and headed off to the coast, with the gale-force winds doing their best to blow us off the road at every gap in the hedges.

Three or four lads in a very big pick-up truck with enormous wheels greeted us on the beach – which was otherwise completely deserted. Such was the sheer force and noise of the wind, we all had to form a sort of huddle and shout at each other to be heard. The guy in charge shouted, 'Right, who wants to go up first?' Well, I knew that after all of Robert's racing accidents he was bolted together like a Meccano set so I volunteered. '100 foot rope or 200 foot rope?' he shouted. I went for the first option.

Soon they began strapping an enormous parachute on to my back. All the straps were the big canvas type, with enormous buckles. There were straps around my chest, waist and legs. I thought I was for the moon rather than the sky. Then they produced a 100 foot, 2 inch thick rope – which was attached to the back of the large pick-up truck – and began tying the other end to the front of my harness, somewhere around the waist area. Robert was inspecting every move and it was then I began to see some concern on his face. 'I'll check the knots, LB,' he shouted into my face. Robert, being a steel erector by trade, was a dab hand at tying knots and it was a relief to me when he said that they were fine.

In normal weather, Robert's words would have been all the reassurance that I needed but the wind was ferocious. We were all having to lean forward into it just to be able to stand upright. The main man then began to give me instructions: 'Right, Liam, we will release the chute and you will take a couple of steps forward and then you will gradually begin to take off. Once you have reached the maximum height, we will drive the pick-up slowly along the full length of the beach. You will be directly connected to the jeep at all times and, when we stop at the far end, you will float gently back to earth.' The head guy (I will never forgive him) checked to see if the team was ready. I took a quick glance at Robert's face, and it was full of trepidation and concern. For a split second I realised this venture was sheer madness, but before I could say 'hold on a minute' the leader shouted, 'Release the chute.'

One of his team was behind me and, before I knew it, I was heading towards outer space quicker than the guy who had connected the Kosangas cooker up wrongly. One of the large thick canvas straps which went from my harness up to the main chute had cut across my face at lift-off and pretty near cut the jaw off me. Before anyone on the ground could say, 'Is he away yet?' I was already at the maximum height of one hundred feet and, but for the fact that I was tied to an enormous pick-up truck, I would have been nothing more than a small dot in the sky. I can remember thinking for a split second, 'Oh boy, the views are superb,' but suddenly I knew something was badly wrong. As I looked down to the beach I could see that everyone (including the experts) were in a state of shock. They hadn't even got into the pick-up truck, such was the panic at seeing me completely out of control, attached to a parachute the size of the roof of the Albert Hall. Suddenly the chute began to weave viciously from side to side with me dangling like a clothes peg, completely helpless, and at the mercy of the man above. I quickly realised that if the parachute leant too far to one side then I would drop to the ground like a stone, and as the swinging from side to side got worse, that is exactly what happened. Suddenly both the enormous chute and I were hurtling downwards. Just before impact I had somehow managed to get my feet down first but on impact I was immediately hammered into the ground like a six-inch nail and then dragged along the beach.

However, before the team of experts or Robert could rescue me, the wind got inside the parachute again and off I went once again towards the clouds at an incredible rate of knots. My back was in agony, but I knew worse was to come. I was staring death in the face and neither I nor anyone on the ground could do anything about it. In no time I was back at 100 feet. Then the swinging from side to side started and the chute and I once again crashed on to the hard sand. This time I wasn't so lucky and I landed practically horizontal, and my head banged the ground at a hell of a speed. The chute dragged me around the beach like a rag doll – I was semi-concussed and to be honest all but ready to give up on any chance of survival.

Then, for the third time, the wind got inside the chute and off I went again, only this time one of the team had managed to grab hold of me as I was taking off. He wrapped his legs and arms around me in an attempt to hold me down, but it was hopeless and as we were about 15 feet up, I remember shouting to him 'Don't be silly, let go,' and he did before the wind took both of us. This time, when I looked down I could see the rear wheels of this brute of a pick-up actually lifting out of the sand. But for the engine, the chances were that the truck I was tied to would have come with me to God knows where.

I was already half knocked out when I once again crashed heavily on to the hard sand and was dragged around. Then everything stopped. I quite honestly thought that I had died, but when I managed to open one eye I saw Robert running towards me as best he could given the injuries he'd sustained in the Isle of Man. He got to me and immediately said, 'Can you hear me, LB? Can you hear me?' I muttered something like, 'Don't touch me, just let me be.' My mouth was full of sand, I remember that. 'Can you move your toes?' was Robert's second question. To our joint relief, I could. Just like in a road racing accident, if the head and spine are relatively unscathed, then the other injuries or breaks should heal in time.

By this time the team of experts had arrived at the scene and I could hear them congratulating Robert. It transpired that Robert had done something he was exceptional at − he had improvised. He had realised that time was running out for me and had decided to head for the parachute in his jeep when it next landed, in an attempt to prevent it from becoming airborne again. He thought that the next crash landing for me would be the last. His only problem was that the chute was dragging me every shape after it, up and down the beach, and at speed into the bargain, which meant that he had to be careful not to drive over me in his attempts to drive over the chute. But he had managed to nail the chute under the wheels of his jeep though the gale was so ferocious that it had ripped the canopy to pieces under the wheels.

There is absolutely no doubt in my mind that Robert's quick thinking saved my life that day, and although I still have the scars and the back pain to this very day, at least I'm still here to tell the tale. Thanks, mate. Anyway, Robert and the others carefully loaded me into Robert's wagon, and as Rob comforted me, young Michael, who could barely reach the pedals, drove us down the beach and towards the nearest hospital, which was Coleraine. I ended up in the fractures clinic at Coleraine hospital, being helped along by Robert and Michael, the complete opposite to the norm, since it was usually me carrying Robert up or down a hospital corridor. The fractures doctor showed me the X-rays and explained to me that I was very lucky as I could so easily have been paralysed or killed. I had crushed a vertebra and fractured my pelvis plus I had suffered severe bruising and a head trauma. It was only when I got home some time later and I was laid up in bed that I could hear Robert in complete convulsions downstairs. Gillian later told me that, as Robert was explaining what had happened, he had gone into a complete kink of laughing and ended up actually rolling around on the floor. If only I could get my hands on the little skitter now.

But it was some time later that the real danger came to light. The team of paraglide experts later told me that their main concern was that I could easily have landed in the sea. The parachute had several heavy straps and buckles and if I had ended up in the water, the chute would have filled up and sucked me under like an anchor. I would have had no chance of undoing the straps. Not long after, tragically, a paraglider did drown in those circumstances, but in a different location. Yes, there's absolutely no doubt in my mind that Robert saved my life that day.

Thirteen
The chequered flag

From the late nineties, with Robert confined to a 125cc machine, and with him now having a home with a proper workshop, it was inevitable that we didn't see as much of each other between races. My cousin Samuel Graham, Uncle Jackie's son, was also very helpful to him during this period, plus his boys William and Michael, and Sam (his brother Jim's son) were all embarking on their own road racing careers – the new generation as they were then. This kept Robert fully occupied and I was delighted to see that he could remain busy in the sport that he loved by not only preparing his own 125cc, but also by helping the boys and passing on his wealth of knowledge to them as they attempted to follow in his footsteps.

But sometimes it's difficult for fathers and sons to communicate, especially when it's the dad telling the boys a few home truths. This became apparent to me when Robert rang me one night from a testing session he was at with William in Spain. 'I just can't get through to him, LB. Do you mind having a word with him? Maybe he'll listen to you.' I said to Robert that I thought that sons don't always like to be told right from wrong, especially by their dads. Perhaps they do listen and pay attention to outsiders, but although Robert may well have thought William wasn't listening, my guess is that deep down Willie knew he was being taught by the best. It's just that acknowledging that from your dad at the time can be difficult.

Of course it was around this time that we were all shattered by some terrible news. I still meet people who recall just where they were and what they were at when they heard that Joey Dunlop had died. The moment I found out is still imprinted on my mind. It was a Sunday around lunchtime and Joey's son Richard was staying at my house. Gillian had just made dinner and Richard had been talking to me about his dad over the meal, and how things had been going for him out in Tallinn in Estonia. Richard and my son William are best mates – they always have been, right the way through from their first day at school together so Richard stayed at our house quite often, and William did the same at Joey's. Richard is a lovely lad, with manners to burn, someone who had the run of our house at any time he wanted, and a lad our family are deeply fond of. When we'd finished eating, Richard and William headed off to play Monopoly. I made my way to our sun lounge with a cup of tea when suddenly I saw a car pull in to our driveway. It's was Joey's daughter Donna with her boyfriend and she was crying sorely. Gillian went to the door to let her in and I heard a commotion up the hall and heard Gillian shouting, 'No, Donna, no.' They appeared at the sun lounge door and Donna said, 'Daddy's dead, Liam.' I was speechless. Just like everyone else who loved Joey, I thought he was bulletproof. Gillian and Donna went to tell Richard. I couldn't bring myself to go with them; I simply couldn't bear the thought of seeing Richard's face when he heard the news. Donna took Richard home with her, but a short time later, they brought him back to us as their house was getting extremely busy and they thought it would be better for

Richard to be somewhere quiet.

A short while later, Gillian shouted to me, 'There's Robert coming in, Liam.' Robert had the freedom of our house, and as the kitchen door opened, there he was, clearly in a severe state of shock. We have a fairly long kitchen and as Robert came in at one end, I was at the other end. As we walked towards each other Robert completely burst out into floods of tears. He semi-collapsed over our range cooker. I threw my arms around him but he was inconsolable. This was the first time I'd ever seen Robert cry – he simply didn't do emotion. Joey meant the world to Robert. The boys' brother Jim appeared and the three of us decided to go somewhere quiet, that's the way they liked to deal with tragedy, so we opted to go to the Ballymoney British Legion Club, into the small private bar they had upstairs, always fairly quiet, especially at that time on a Sunday.

Only a handful of people were there and when they heard the news they were polite and didn't bother the lads. We only stayed about an hour. It was the most surreal time I can remember. None of us could comprehend that the greatest road racer of all time was gone, never again to grace the circuits he had ridden with such success and modesty for countless years.

Joey's funeral was the biggest our town had ever seen or ever will. The entire country and beyond were heartbroken. So many people had lost their all-time hero and Robert was no different, hand on heart. He knew he had to appear to be strong for his family, but I still feel to this day that Robert never ever got over Joey's death. Robert's love, admiration and respect for Joey were comparable to the strongest I've ever witnessed between two brothers in my entire life. Joey was a one-off, never to be repeated. That bright light which always guided and steered Robert, extinguished for ever and a day.

To me anyhow, after Joey's death, Robert never seemed quite

the same. At this time I genuinely felt that he would just finish his career taking the wee 125cc lady out in selective races and would spend most of his time schooling the young Dunlop lads. Alas, for the umpteenth time, I completely underestimated the Dunlop mentality. Rob retire? Not a hope in hell.

Robert proved to everyone that he could still cut it at the highest level, albeit in the less glamorous 125cc class, when he won his fifteenth and final race at the North West 200 in 2006. It was a victory that didn't come easy as Robert was forced to draw on his vast reserves of experience and skill to reel in long-time leader Michael Wilcox before putting a pass on the English rider at the final chicane on the last lap, snatching victory by a whisker. It was yet another astonishing feat in the career of Robert Dunlop, but sadly this would prove to be his crowning glory at the event where he had enjoyed so many of the stand-out triumphs of his glittering career. It is testament to the greatness of the man that his record still stands. His final win in 2006 was his only success at the North West 200 in the years after his accident and I have absolutely no doubt he could have doubled that record tally but for his career-changing injuries and his untimely death.

Robert lost his life at the North West 200 – the race he loved more than any other, on the very course where he had dominated for so many years in front of thousands of adoring fans. Rob had a conscience and was always aware of how much his true fans wanted to see him compete and continue to be successful. Even when his machinery would not have been the most competitive or when his battle wounds were beginning to play up, he still felt the need to pull on his leathers and helmet and give of his best for his fans, the Dunlop name and himself.

On 15 May 2008, Robert had entered the 125cc race as usual but he had also decided to compete on a larger 250cc two-stroke Honda owned by Antrim businessman Roy Hanna. I was shocked by this decision and I was also a bit cross with Robert as well. I felt that a 250cc machine was too much for him to take on. Rob felt differently, though, and I believe he thought the line-up for the 250cc race that year was weaker than it had been in previous seasons and saw an opportunity to take advantage. He was also aware that other riders were beginning to close in on his record and felt he had a good chance of adding to his haul of fifteen wins on Roy Hanna's machine. Rob's sons, William and Michael, were also entered in the same class and in my opinion it was odds-on that it was one of his two boys – now emerging talents in their own right, William in particular at this point – who would take all the beating. I arrived late on the Thursday evening ahead of the final practice sessions and Rob's 250cc Honda was being prepared by Roy Hanna's team. After hanging around in the paddock for a while I decided to make my way down to York Corner. I'd agreed with Robert that I would monitor his braking points, conscious that for some years now Rob was only used to having a braking marker for the slower 125cc machine. Given the extra speed of the bigger two-stroke machine, I was keen to keep a watchful eye and relay any information I thought might be helpful back to Robert after the session. I had literally just arrived at my vantage point when the practice was stopped on the first lap due to a red-flag incident. As I waited for the session to be re-started, my phone rang and on the other end was the unmistakable voice of my old friend and Rob's former sponsor PJ O'Kane, who said, 'I hear it's Robert who's come off at Mather's, LB, and apparently it's a bad one.' The infamous Mather's Cross section of the North West 200 course was still a flat-out right-hander on a two-stroke machine in 2008. It wasn't a place where you wanted to come off and my heart sank at PJ's news. I can't explain why, but a cold feeling came over me, a sensation unrelated to the chilly air coming off the North Atlantic ocean that night, and my instinct told me I needed to make my way to the hospital. I set off immediately on my own on the short drive to the Causeway Hospital in

Coleraine, which is about ten minutes away from Portstewart.

By the time I arrived at the A&E Department I could sense that it was serious and I knew too that it was Robert. The ambulance was parked up outside with the two rear doors wide open when I got there but Rob had already been rushed into theatre. Suddenly, worried faces appeared from everywhere and people were running about crying. I made my way outside and sat down on a small wall outside at the entrance to the car park to gather myself. I was stunned and I felt numb, but I told myself that Robert was invincible – he wouldn't die and he wouldn't go without saying goodbye. I thought about all that we had been through together and took comfort from the fact that he had almost been killed before at the TT, yet somehow he pulled through and I felt at that moment that he would do so again: 'He'll be okay,' I reassured myself. As members of the Dunlop family began arriving at the hospital I still stayed in the background, believing – or in hindsight kidding myself – that there was no real need to panic just yet. Then I saw that Robert's wife Louise and his mum May had arrived and I really started to worry. A short time later Robert's brother-in-law, Jim Stevenson, appeared out the door of A&E and waved me over before breaking the news I never thought I'd hear. 'It's all over, Liam. He's gone – Robert's dead.' I nearly collapsed on the spot. And I just couldn't take it in. Jim was telling me that I was to come inside to go and see Robert in the trauma theatre room but my head was spinning and I felt like I was on autopilot. I followed him and we made our way there, my stomach aching as Jim opened the door and we stepped inside. Robert was laid out flat on the table, still in his racing leathers. After a brief pause, I walked over to him and held his hand, which was still warm. He had a slight, peaceful smile on his face, which was thankfully unmarked. I just wanted to pick him up, carry him home and make him better again. My heart was in pieces. This time, there would be no comeback for the racing gladiator and

I felt crushed as the weight of that horrifying reality sunk in. As I stood there holding his right hand I noticed that a couple of his knuckles were skinned where they had obviously struck the road. The tears streamed down my face and there was nothing I could do to hold them back: the kid brother I never had was gone. I half expected Rob to open his eyes, wink at me and say, 'I had you fooled there, LB.' But I knew it was over and I gave his hand a squeeze and left. We were directed to a family room where Robert's nearest and dearest had assembled. The Dunlop family are such a modest, humble dynasty, no different in many respects to any other normal family, and it destroyed me to see these ordinary country people in absolute pieces, torn to shreds by Robert's death. Each of us were inconsolable and I felt myself questioning my own religious beliefs in that moment, wondering how something so awful could happen yet again to such a decent family.

I rang home and broke the terrible news to my wife Gillian who was distraught. My next call was to my very close friend, Jackie Fullerton; someone who was held in the highest esteem by both Robert and Joey. He could barely take in what I was telling him and actually had to ring me back to enquire what exactly had happened to Robert, such was his initial shock. Still in a daze, I ventured back outside the hospital once more into the public car park. Within minutes, I was met by PJ O'Kane and his close friend Patsy Deighan. The big man was beside himself with grief, pitching between disbelief and absolute anguish. By now, anger had set in for me and I was cursing to myself inside, asking why the hell he had been out there on a 250 in the first place; and wondering what on earth had happened.

Right then, though, was no time for such questions and I tried to pull myself together and focus on the much more important matters at hand. My immediate concern was for Louise and their three sons, William, Michael and Daniel, and Rob's mother May. William and Michael were of course well known within

Northern Ireland sporting circles but the wider public knew little about Daniel, who was serving with the British Army in Afghanistan. God help May because she had lost her husband Willie a short time before and, of course, had experienced the loss of a son already. I kept thinking about how much she had been through and wondering how she would possibly cope with another shattering loss.

I spent the next few dark days at Robert's home on the Lisboy Road, outside the townland of Killyrammer. The family rallied round one another, as they always did, and Louise was doing her best to get through each hour as well as she could despite her obvious distress. William stayed out in the garage most of the time, shutting himself away from the hordes of visitors arriving to pay their respects; it was his way of handling the grief. The lad was simply unable to face people, particularly those he didn't particularly know. I went outside to see him, gave him a wee squeeze, and said, 'God bless son', and just left him to it; he wanted to grieve in private and I wasn't going to intrude. Michael, who is four years younger than William, approached the situation differently and was very hands on, taking it upon himself to handle all the arrangements that needed to be attended to at the time of a funeral. He handled those decisions superbly and I commend him for that. Daniel arrived home at the first opportunity and the whole family was united in their grief. I was appointed by the family to liaise with the Police Service of Northern Ireland, the undertakers and Ballymoney Borough Council on the matters that had arisen from Robert's untimely passing. He was to be buried at Garryduff Presbyterian Church, where his brother Joey had been laid to rest eight years earlier, and – with many thousands of mourners expected – it was my job to issue tickets granting access to the church to those selected by the family. Obviously, the family were all to be seated at the front, and then I identified those close friends, colleagues, members of the media and sponsors who should be considered for the limited places available inside the small country church. I was also requested to be at the house when the undertakers brought Robert home from the funeral parlour.

When the call came through that Robert was about to leave Ballymoney, which was a journey of approximately fifteen minutes, we assembled in the back yard with a clear view of the approach lane. Before long the black hearse appeared and it was an overpowering moment as we watched it slowly drive towards us, painfully aware that this was the final time the 'Micro' would be coming home. We brought Robert in through the front door and I helped the undertaker carry him upstairs to a bedroom and then we left until they removed the lid of the coffin. Everyone at the house took it in turns to go up to see Robert one final time and after each member of his family had spent some moments with him, I was invited to go upstairs and say one last goodbye. One memory that has always stuck with me from that day was how contented Robert looked, more so than I had ever seen him when he was alive. To me, he was just asleep.

I was kept busy in the days leading up to Robert's funeral, meeting with the police to discuss traffic arrangements and funeral times and looking after some of the peripheral details to give the family time to mourn their loss. One of the more delicate matters was accommodating the visits of the First and Deputy First Ministers of Northern Ireland, who at the time were Ian Paisley and Martin McGuinness. Ballymoney Council had approached me to ask me if I would liaise with both men, who wanted to come to the house and pay their respects. The Dunlop door was open to everyone regardless of their religious affiliation and no one within the family had a sectarian bone in their body. Their attitude was that if someone wanted to come and say goodbye to Robert, they were more than welcome. I had no concerns over the visit of Ian Paisley, who hailed from the north Antrim area where the Dunlop family and I myself lived, which has a unionist majority. However, I was obviously alert to the fact that Martin McGuinness was a Sinn Féin leader and I admit to having slight reservations over the type of reception he might receive in what was a unionist heartland. This was no time for politics though and I just got on with the job at hand. It was agreed that both men would attend the house at the same time. Ian Paisley knew where Robert lived and he decided to make his own way there. Martin McGuinness had no idea where the family home was located and therefore it was arranged that I would travel to meet him on the outskirts of Ballymoney and accompany him to Robert's home. We parked up in the packed yard and as I walked with him towards the house you could have heard a pin drop. I took him into the large kitchen area and introduced him to the various family members before being informed that Dr Paisley was present in a small, private sitting room at the rear of the house. I thought it would be best if I guided Martin to see his political colleague and once we arrived, they both took a seat on the same sofa and I left them to it.

I tried to keep myself fully occupied during these days as it helped me not to think too much about the dreaded moment when we would all lay our hands on Robert for the last time ever. Throughout the wake, William largely remained outside in the garage, working away on his bikes. His family were of the opinion that he intended to ride in the 250cc race at the North West 200 on the Saturday, less than two days after Robert's fatal crash. I felt that William was simply locking himself away to deal with his grief and I didn't for one moment consider that he genuinely intended to race. For Michael, racing seemed to be the furthest thing from his mind but then on the Saturday morning of the North West – one day before their dad was due to be buried – I received a phone call from Louise who said, 'You'd better get down to the North West, Liam. William and Michael are both away.' I was stunned but I set off like a scalded cat and reached the seaside resort of Portstewart, which was absolutely jam-packed, as it always is on race day. I abandoned my car and made a run for the paddock at the start and finish area on the Coast Road. As I ran along Portstewart Golf Course, which was lined with thousands of spectators along the road from Primrose Corner down to York hairpin, my mind was racing and it soon dawned on me from the fevered commentary booming out from the PA system that the 250cc race was underway. I thought I was hearing things when the commentator announced that Michael was fighting for the lead with John McGuinness. The crowd was hysterical and the goose bumps were tingling on the back of my neck. Out of breath, I arrived at the start and finish area and the fans, who were bunched up six-deep, spotted me and moved aside to let me clamber over the fence. I actually fell on to the road in my haste. At this point Michael was leading from English rider Christian Elkin at the Juniper Hill chicane on the final lap. In the nick of time, I had made it to see him cross the line and take the chequered flag to win the 250cc race at the North West 200, the same class that had claimed the life of his father not even two days earlier.

It was an astonishing achievement and the ultimate tribute to Robert on one of the most emotional days ever witnessed in the history of the famous Irish road race. No one who was present that day will ever forget what they witnessed and there wasn't a dry eye in the house. In terms of all-time Northern Ireland sporting achievements, this must go down as the greatest and most unique. All the talk had centred on the likelihood of William racing, and indeed it had been his intention to compete, but he was ruled out with a mechanical problem with his machine on the warm-up lap. Michael had made a last-minute decision to race and had gone out and delivered the goods against unimaginable odds; it was a story worthy of a Hollywood script. The race organiser, Mervyn Whyte, had told me the day prior to the race that he doubted William would be allowed to race give the circumstances because the race committee were of the opinion that he wouldn't be in the right frame of mind or properly focused to race at high speeds. I remember telling Mervyn not to worry, that I doubted either of the boys would turn up to race; after all my years of experience at Robert's side, you'd think I should have known better. To turn up at a world-class major international road race and actually win, never mind compete, when his father was lying at home in a coffin was an unimaginable feat and words still fail me to this day to describe what that young lad achieved under such terrible circumstances. He was driven on by sheer, raw emotion and a determination to win the race for his dad, who believed the 250cc race trophy that year had a Dunlop's name on it; it was absolutely mind-blowing and the events of that day temporarily lightened the burden of Rob's death for everyone, but the elation of that incredible moment soon petered out and it was back to reality as we returned to the family home.

The day after the race, Robert left us for the final time. The house was crammed with mourners and the undertakers gave the dreaded signal that it was time to go. The last private words were uttered by his closest family as they said goodbye to their daddy, husband, brother and son and I remember that empty feeling in the pit of my stomach as it sunk in that I would never see Robert again: not in this life anyhow. My own house was packed that morning with my family and a few members of the Northern Ireland media, and others had arranged to meet us at the church. Robert was extremely popular with the media and there was a large turnout of journalists. He always said what he felt and was confident in front of the camera, and the press loved that.

Thousands turned out to pay their respects and Robert's funeral was the second biggest I have ever attended. He was laid to rest in the graveyard adjoining Garryduff Church, beside Joey. It was a tremendous show of respect for Rob, with young and old, Protestant and Catholic united in their grief. His loss left a huge void in so many lives and I was no different. Michael had asked me if I would speak at the funeral and I initially apologised and said that I couldn't because I knew I would break down, but he asked me again early on the morning of the funeral and this time I was unable to say no. I sat down in my sun lounge and penned a wee poem.

The Micro

'Twas a bright and sunny evening,
The fifteenth of May,
When the good Lord our Saviour,
called you away.
I wasn't quite ready,
It seemed very soon,
A terrible shock to the folk from the Toon.
But typical Robert,
You didn't let us know,
You'd done a deal with God,
It was your time to go.
If ye could just see how many,
Have come to say goodbye,
You'd now understand,
That it's okay to cry.
But we'll get through this,
Don't ask me how,
But the memories you've left us,
Will do us for now.
To your family and me,
You were always the 'wean',
Let's hope that some day,
We'll all meet again.

Fourteen
Gone but not forgotten

After Robert's death, I wasn't convinced I'd ever feel the same again about road racing, and I wasn't someone who could just jump ship and put my support behind someone else and move on. However, with two of Robert's three sons still racing now I take a big-time interest in both their careers – and they have certainly lived up to the Dunlop name, winning at all the major international road races and putting themselves at the top of their chosen profession. They can both look after themselves, but they know I am here for them if they ever need my advice.

Very soon after Robert's passing I was contacted by the then Ballymoney Borough Council and asked to act as liaison between the council and the Dunlop family with regard to some form of permanent memorial to Robert. This eventually took the form of a wonderful memorial garden, created directly beside Joey's, at the foot of the town's main street. The council also informed me that if we (Robert's family and friends) would like to have a bronze sculpture of Robert erected in the new memorial garden, then we would have to fund this ourselves, through public subscription. So we set up a fund-raising steering committee, and with the incredible generosity of the public, we were soon able to commission the Scottish sculptor David Annand to create the bronze sculpture of Robert that now stands proudly in his memorial garden. Robert's pose for the sculpture was chosen by Louise – it's one she always liked – and I must say that I agreed wholeheartedly with her choice, especially given that in the sculpture, Rob is sporting his trademark cheeky grin. I must commend the then Ballymoney Council for the manner in which they conducted the entire memorial garden project. They recognised Joey's and Robert's tremendous contribution to making our small town of Ballymoney world famous. The Dunlop boys had done their bit, and our council certainly did their bit to ensure both boys will be remembered for ever by everyone. The Dunlop memorial gardens are now a Mecca each road racing season for thousands of fans who call to pay their respects to two road racing legends.

Robert's family and my family have remained very close friends. I suppose the joys and heartbreak we all shared has really cemented a friendship that will stand the test of time. My admiration and respect for them will never waver.

At the time of Robert's death I was managing Institute Football Club in Londonderry and, before he died, he kept in touch regularly for an update on how things were going. He liked the football as well. It was also around this time that I began to do little bits of sport punditry and analysis for BBC Radio Ulster and as time went by I found myself being used pretty regularly by the Beeb to commentate not only on football but also on the motorcycle road races. That progressed to me being asked to do course commentaries at various national road races not covered by BBC Radio Ulster. Hosting dinners and after dinner speaking also somehow entered my diary and with my broad north Antrim accent, that's still one I find hard to fathom. Also for the past six years, I have been a sports columnist for the *News Letter*. I'm extremely honoured to be an ambassador for Samaritans, a patron for the Compass Advocacy Network for people with learning difficulties, and a patron for the Harry Gregg football foundation, which supports children in football.

I often wonder what Robert would have made of my career now, and I genuinely think he would have been pretty proud of me. He would also have been there at the drop of a hat to give me a hand if needed. Yes, I have no doubt that the younger brother I never had would have accompanied me to many of the events I attend, probably with that favourite old UB40 tape of his blasting out non stop, as it always did when we were on the road. I still miss him, and I guess I always will. We had a special bond, which doesn't come along very often. He was a winner and he always will be in my eyes. RIP, Rob.

Acknowledgements

There are many people who I would like to thank for their help with this book – Gavan Caldwell for the front cover photograph; Baylon McCaughey and everyone else who contributed photographs for the picture section; Deric Henderson; Adrian Logan; the Dunlop family, and Louise Dunlop in particular; Patsy, Helen and Jim at Blackstaff Press; and all my family and friends.

I would like to give a special note of thanks to journalist and motorcycle expert Kyle White, who was involved with this project from the very beginning, and who had the unenviable job of typing up many, many handwritten sheets and helping me to shape the story. Without Kyle's expertise, patience and research skills, I would have given up halfway through. He was a massive help from start to finish. Thanks, Kyle.

If you enjoyed *Full Throttle*,
look out for

OLD SCHOOL

BECKETT, BIKES, BALLS & ALL

Liam Beckett

Following on from the success of his bestselling book, *Full Throttle*,
Liam Beckett, one of Northern Ireland's best-loved sports pundits,
talks frankly about his life in football and road racing and what
these sports mean to him.

Full of funny stories, honesty and warmth, and served with a good
dose of straight-talking, this is vintage Beckett, telling it like it is.

For more information visit:
www.blackstaffpress.com

and follow Liam at:

 @liam_beckett